Too Many Goodbyes

THE AZRIELI SERIES OF HOLOCAUST SURVIVOR MEMOIRS: PUBLISHED TITLES

ENGLISH TITLES

Judy Abrams, *Tenuous Threads*/ Eva Felsenburg Marx, *One of the Lucky Ones*

Amek Adler, *Six Lost Years*

Molly Applebaum, *Buried Words*

Claire Baum, *The Hidden Package*

Bronia and Joseph Beker, *Joy Runs Deeper*

Tibor Benyovits, *Unsung Heroes*

Max Bornstein, *If Home Is Not Here*

Felicia Carmelly, *Across the Rivers of Memory*

Tommy Dick, *Getting Out Alive*

Marian Domanski, *Fleeing from the Hunter*

Anita Ekstein, *Always Remember Who You Are*

John Freund, *Spring's End*

Myrna Goldenberg (Editor), *Before All Memory Is Lost: Women's Voices from the Holocaust*

René Goldman, *A Childhood Adrift*

Elly Gotz, *Flights of Spirit*

Ibolya Grossman and Andy Réti, *Stronger Together*

Pinchas Gutter, *Memories in Focus*

Anna Molnár Hegedűs, *As the Lilacs Bloomed*

Rabbi Pinchas Hirschprung, *The Vale of Tears*

Bronia Jablon, *A Part of Me*

Helena Jockel, *We Sang in Hushed Voices*

Eddie Klein, *Inside the Walls*

Michael Kutz, *If, By Miracle*

Nate Leipciger, *The Weight of Freedom*

Alex Levin, *Under the Yellow and Red Stars*

Fred Mann, *A Drastic Turn of Destiny*

Michael Mason, *A Name Unbroken*

Leslie Meisels with Eva Meisels, *Suddenly the Shadow Fell*

Leslie Mezei, *A Tapestry of Survival*

Muguette Myers, *Where Courage Lives*

David Newman, *Hope's Reprise*

Arthur Ney, *W Hour*

Felix Opatowski, *Gatehouse to Hell*

Marguerite Élias Quddus, *In Hiding*

Maya Rakitova, *Behind the Red Curtain*

Henia Reinhartz, *Bits and Pieces*

Betty Rich, *Little Girl Lost*

Paul-Henri Rips, *E/96: Fate Undecided*

Margrit Rosenberg Stenge, *Silent Refuge*

Steve Rotschild, *Traces of What Was*

Judith Rubinstein, *Dignity Endures*

Martha Salcudean, *In Search of Light*

Kitty Salsberg and Ellen Foster, *Never Far Apart*

Joseph Schwarzberg, *Dangerous Measures*

Zuzana Sermer, *Survival Kit*

Rachel Shtibel, *The Violin*/ Adam Shtibel, *A Child's Testimony*

Maxwell Smart, *Chaos to Canvas*

Gerta Solan, *My Heart Is At Ease*

Zsuzsanna Fischer Spiro, *In Fragile Moments*/ Eva Shainblum, *The Last Time*

George Stern, *Vanished Boyhood*

Willie Sterner, *The Shadows Behind Me*

Ann Szedlecki, *Album of My Life*

William Tannenzapf, *Memories from the Abyss*/ Renate Krakauer, *But I Had a Happy Childhood*

Elsa Thon, *If Only It Were Fiction*

Agnes Tomasov, *From Generation to Generation*

Joseph Tomasov, *From Loss to Liberation*

Sam Weisberg, *Carry the Torch*/ Johnny Jablon, *A Lasting Legacy*

Leslie Vertes, *Alone in the Storm*

Anka Voticky, *Knocking on Every Door*

Too Many Goodbyes:
The Diaries of Susan Garfield

Susan Garfield

THE AZRIELI FOUNDATION · www.azrielifoundation.org

Cover and book design by Mark Goldstein · Map on page xxxi by François Blanc
Family tree on pages xxxii–xxxiii by Keaton Taylor · Endpaper maps by Martin Gilbert

Translation of Endre Ady's poem "I Should Love to Be Loved" by Eli Siegel on page xxxvii reprinted with permission from Definition Press. (*Hail, American Development.* New York: Definition Press, 1968. Page 80.)
    Translation of Susan Garfield's 1944 diary and postcards on pages 1–12 and 162–171 by Marietta Morry and Lynda Muir. Translation of Susan Garfield's 1947 and 1948–1950 diaries by Susan Garfield. Susan's translation of her 1944 and 1947 diaries was first published in *Voices of Winnipeg Holocaust Survivors*, ed. Belle Millo (Jarniewski) (Winnipeg, 2010), 79–89.

LIBRARY AND ARCHIVES CANADA CATALOGUING IN PUBLICATION

Garfield, Susan, 1933– author. Too Many Goodbyes: The Diaries of Susan Garfield/ Susan Garfield

(Azrieli series of Holocaust survivor memoirs. Series XII)
Includes bibliographical references and index. Canadiana 20190216670
ISBN 978-1-988065-55-7 (softcover) · 8 7 6 5 4 3 2 1

LCSH: Garfield, Susan, 1933- — Diaries. LCSH: Jews — Hungary — Budapest — Diaries. LCSH: Jews, Hungarian — Canada — Diaries. LCSH: Holocaust survivors — Hungary — Budapest — Diaries. LCSH: Holocaust, Jewish (1939–1945) — Hungary — Budapest. LCSH: World War, 1939–1945 — Hungary — Budapest. LCSH: Budapest (Hungary) — Biography. LCGFT: Autobiographies.

DS135.H93 G37 2019   DDC 943.9/004924 — DC23

PRINTED IN CANADA

The Azrieli Series of Holocaust Survivor Memoirs

Naomi Azrieli, Publisher

Jody Spiegel, Program Director
Arielle Berger, Managing Editor
Matt Carrington, Editor
Devora Levin, Assistant Editor
Elizabeth Lasserre, Senior Editor, French-Language Editions
Elin Beaumont, Community and Education Initiatives
Catherine Person, Education and Academic Initiatives/French Editor
Stephanie Corazza, Academic and Education Initiatives
Marc-Olivier Cloutier, School and Education Initiatives
Elizabeth Banks, Digital Asset Curator and Archivist
Catherine Quintal, Digital Communications Assistant

Mark Goldstein, Art Director
François Blanc, Cartographer
Bruno Paradis, Layout, French-Language Editions

Contents

Series Preface:
In their own words. . .

In telling these stories, the writers have liberated themselves. For so many years we did not speak about it, even when we became free people living in a free society. Now, when at last we are writing about what happened to us in this dark period of history, knowing that our stories will be read and live on, it is possible for us to feel truly free. These unique historical documents put a face on what was lost, and allow readers to grasp the enormity of what happened to six million Jews — one story at a time.

    David J. Azrieli, C.M., C.Q., M.Arch
    Holocaust survivor and founder, The Azrieli Foundation

Since the end of World War II, approximately 40,000 Jewish Holocaust survivors have immigrated to Canada. Who they are, where they came from, what they experienced and how they built new lives for themselves and their families are important parts of our Canadian heritage. The Azrieli Foundation's Holocaust Survivor Memoirs Program was established in 2005 to preserve and share the memoirs written by those who survived the twentieth-century Nazi genocide of the Jews of Europe and later made their way to Canada. The memoirs encourage readers to engage thoughtfully and critically with the complexities of the Holocaust and to create meaningful connections with the lives of survivors.

Millions of individual stories are lost to us forever. By preserving the stories written by survivors and making them widely available to a broad audience, the Azrieli Foundation's Holocaust Survivor Memoirs Program seeks to sustain the memory of all those who perished at the hands of hatred, abetted by indifference and apathy. The personal accounts of those who survived against all odds are as different as the people who wrote them, but all demonstrate the courage, strength, wit and luck that it took to prevail and survive in such terrible adversity. The memoirs are also moving tributes to people — strangers and friends — who risked their lives to help others, and who, through acts of kindness and decency in the darkest of moments, frequently helped the persecuted maintain faith in humanity and courage to endure. These accounts offer inspiration to all, as does the survivors' desire to share their experiences so that new generations can learn from them.

The Holocaust Survivor Memoirs Program collects, archives and publishes select survivor memoirs and makes the print editions available free of charge to educational institutions and Holocaust-education programs across Canada. They are also available for sale online to the general public. All revenues to the Azrieli Foundation from the sales of the Azrieli Series of Holocaust Survivor Memoirs go toward the publishing and educational work of the memoirs program.

~

The Azrieli Foundation would like to express appreciation to the following people for their invaluable efforts in producing this book: Doris Bergen, Mark Duffus (Maracle Inc), Farla Klaiman, Susan Roitman, Stephen Ullstrom, and Margie Wolfe & Emma Rodgers of Second Story Press. We are also grateful to Belle Jarniewski for giving us permission to reprint Susan Garfield's 1947 diary excerpt, which gives a taste of her story and first appeared in *Voices of Winnipeg Holocaust Survivors* (2010).

About the Footnotes and Glossary

The following memoir contains a number of terms, concepts and historical references that may be unfamiliar to the reader. The editor has added footnotes relevant to the memoir, and explanations of some terms were generated from the Azrieli Foundation's extensive glossary. For general information on major organizations; significant historical events and people; geographical locations; religious and cultural terms; and foreign-language words and expressions that will help give context and background to the events described in the text, please see the glossary beginning on page 153.

Introduction

In January 1947, Zsuzsanna Löffler, a native of Budapest, Hungary, composed a final passage in her wartime diary. With an air of sadness, the passage hinted at big changes for the then thirteen-year-old:

Why do I want to go to Canada? Only sad memories bind me to Hungary. It will be painful to leave my relatives, aunts, grandparents and cousins who love me and who don't dare detain me for fear of reproach in the future. My utmost desire is to leave, and I would consider myself unfortunate if I would not be successful in this. I do not wish to live in a place where everything I see awakens memories and tears at healing wounds. Here everything drags me backwards — the past, the people. Only in a new environment, far from here, can I look forward to the future.

Recorded after a two-year hiatus from writing, Zsuzsanna's remarks bear little resemblance to those noted by her younger self. Gone is the self-centred, independent child with dreams of attending *gimnázium* (high school). In its place: an orphaned survivor who lost her home, sense of security and parents during the Holocaust. All hopes for the future lay outside of Hungary in a distant country called Canada. Yet, the trauma and losses of Zsuzsanna's past remained her constant shadow as she embarked on her new life in western Canada, living with her new adopted name, Susan.

Too Many Goodbyes: The Diaries of Susan Garfield poignantly articulates the memories, trauma and determination of a lone young Hungarian teenager child who survived the Holocaust. The book is divided into two distinct sections: diary and memoir. Susan's Budapest diary chapters, written in Hungarian from June to November 1944, and restarted in January 1947, chronicle the family's experiences in wartime Hungary. Whereas the 1944 diary includes frequent separate entries, Susan wrote the 1947 diary as a single entry, lengthy autobiography in anticipation of a move to Canada and the promise of adoption and so-called "life of a princess." Though written against the backdrop of intense warfare and following the loss of her father, Susan's 1944 entries exude a sense of optimism and confidence for the future. By 1947, despite her pending immigration to a family in Canada, this optimism had been replaced by despondency: "The gap that exists in time is best left unfilled, as it contains neither joy nor beauty, but death, fear of death and fathomless pain. My dear Father, my dear Mother, you are no more. No one on earth will ever know my feelings about this."

This sentiment continues to prevail throughout the 1948–1949 and 1949–1950 chapters of Susan's diary. These entries follow her resettlement in western Canada, first in Vegreville, Alberta, as the foster daughter of the Kleins, a well-meaning Canadian Jewish couple. Susan demonstrated academic prowess, winning an essay-writing contest during her first year in an English-language school. Yet, scholarly achievements could not alleviate the solitude Susan felt in this rural community, eons away from her cultured upbringing in Budapest. After failed attempts to seek transfer to Toronto, Ontario, home to a substantial Hungarian Jewish community, Susan was resettled in Winnipeg, Manitoba. Having willingly given up free room and board by leaving the Kleins, Susan was forced to accept work as an exploited housekeeper, child caregiver and shop attendant to cover her living expenses while she completed high school. Despite the presence of refugee friends and a cousin the Kleins had assisted in immigrating from Hungary, Susan's sadness and desperation to return "home" to her family in Budapest persisted throughout her journey.

Ultimately, while Canada presented Susan with the opportunity to move beyond the devastation and wartime memories of Hungary, she also experienced a high degree of culture shock and abject loneliness as a teenage immigrant, and the feeling that nobody loved or cared for her. This disheartenment flows throughout the second part of *Too Many Goodbyes*, a reflective memoir written intermittently decades after the Holocaust.

Three themes are peppered throughout the diary and memoir: loss, love and home. The narrative begins with Susan's earliest losses, starting with two painful goodbyes with her father, then the news of his eventual "disappearance" deep inside the Soviet Union. A series of anti-Jewish decrees stole Susan's freedom, followed in quick succession by her mother's sudden departure, the loss of her childhood home and the loss of economic stability. Liberation brought with it the tragic confirmation of her mother's death. "Things were just not the same in my family after the war. Beloved members of the family were gone."

Susan's search for home and love, too, defined her life. Leaving Hungary and a caring, doting family to become an immigrant in Canada stripped Susan of her sense of belonging to — and in — a place. Budapest, a place where she could no longer live, nevertheless remained 'home.' In her pursuit of love and belonging, Susan attempted to fill a void created by the Holocaust and the trauma she survived in its aftermath. Susan's memoir offers a heartbreaking lens into the private experiences of one war orphan on her journey to redefine herself after so many goodbyes.

$\sim$

"At such an early age, I was deprived of love, security and comfort — little by little, year by year. First by my father — saying goodbye to him at age nine is seared into my brain. Then my mother, when she left me alone at a time of extreme danger. Recalling my goodbye with my father, I knew then that there was a possibility of my mother being gone from me forever. As a child, I realized the precariousness of my own life."

Zsuzsanna Veronika Löffler was born in Budapest on June 3, 1933, the adored only child of Magdolna (née Weisz) and Bernat Löffler. Susan's 1944 diary recounts happy memories of a little girl, "spoiled as only children often are." The centre of her parents' universe, Susie, as she was known to friends and family, enjoyed a comfortable up-bringing in a two-bedroom apartment within walking distance of her extended family. Weekends were dedicated to family time: dinners with her grandparents; card nights with aunts, uncles and cousins; and adventures in the countryside. Young Susie shared a special bond with her father, an outgoing amateur actor who wrote poetry. The two occasionally visited the cinema to see American films like *The Wizard of Oz* and *The Blue Bird*. Susie's excitement grew whenever the MGM lion appeared and roared on the film screen.

Susie preferred to spend time socializing and performing plays with cousins and neighbourhood girls rather than studying. Susie's parents nurtured their daughter's independent spirit and self-reliance by permitting her to explore the city, embracing its nooks and crannies. (A deep attachment to Budapest — the neighbourhoods, the culture, the energy — remains decades after immigrating to Canada.) Susie's knowledge of the city, combined with her fierce spirit, would later aid her survival.

Although Bernat and Magda Löffler had instilled strong, independent values and confidence in their daughter, they also succeeded in shielding her from the political rumblings that grew louder in Hungary by the day. The multiple and overlapping international crises emanating from World War I — and the events that followed — culminated in simmering tensions throughout Europe.

The post-war period was coloured by mass upheaval and a refugee crisis. Treaties imposed on the defeated nations by the Allied powers caused the reconstitution of national borders. The Treaty of Versailles (June 28, 1919) left a devastating mark on Germany. Demands for reparation payments, the forced acceptance of the "war guilt" clause, the dismantling of the army and significant territorial losses contributed to tumultuous conditions for Germans. An upswing in popular support for nationalist right-wing politics culminated in Adolf Hitler's National Socialist German Workers' Party (Nazi Party) coming to power in 1933. The ramifications of Hitler's appointment as chancellor extended far beyond Germany's borders. Among the countries caught up in this tectonic shift in European politics was Hungary.

The Austro-Hungarian Empire experienced complete dissolution resulting from its participation on the defeated side in World War I. The conditions set in the June 1920 Treaty of Trianon substantially diminished Hungary's physical size, with 60 per cent of its pre-war territory relinquished to the new state, Czechoslovakia. The new, independent and ethnically diverse Hungary drove nationalists into a state of despair. In 1935, Hungarian fascist leader Ferenc Szálasi capitalized on the country's internal chaos; in 1939, he combined four fascist groups to form the Party of National Will, renamed the Arrow Cross Party. Modelled on the Nazi Party, the pan-national, anti-Communist and antisemitic Arrow Cross Party became the official opposition in parliament by Susie's sixth birthday, endangering not only her idyllic childhood but the safety of her family and Hungarian Jewry writ large.

As nativism took hold across Hungary, so too did assimilation, high rates of intermarriage and rising conversions among the country's urban Jews. This caused considerable rifts between observant elders and their more secular offspring, even in the most progressive Budapest Jewish households. Susie witnessed such tensions firsthand when her maternal aunt, Bözsi (Erzsebet) Weisz, became engaged to Sandor Nagy, a Christian man. Upon hearing the news of the pending union, her grandparents threatened to sit shiva unless future children were raised as Jews. The couple fulfilled this commitment; more significantly, Sandor's Christianity helped save his nuclear family — as well as Bözsi's niece, Susie — during the Nazi occupation of Budapest.

Various rationalizations were proffered for Hungarian Jews seeking conversion or intermarriage. Jews faced overt antisemitism and *numerus clausus* that limited participation in higher education and specific industries. Susie's father, Bernat, experienced such discrimination firsthand: when the quota system precluded his pursuit of studying medicine, he instead established a typewriter company. Bernat ran the business from the family apartment until his conscription for labour service in 1942, at which time his wife, Magda, took over the operations.

Until Bernat's departure, Susie remained oblivious to the declining situation for Hungary's Jewish population. Organized attacks on Jewish communities in the provinces corresponded to the strengthening of German-Hungarian relations. In an effort to solidify this alliance, Germany orchestrated the recovery of Hungarian-speaking regions in Slovakia and Carpatho-Ukraine ceded to Czechoslovakia according to the Treaty of Trianon. Germany's bets were well-hedged. In November 1940, Hungary officially joined the Axis alliance.[1]

Anti-Jewish decrees aimed at eliminating threats to Hungary's national values pre-empted the Hungarian regime's alliance with Hitler. The first decree, issued on May 28, 1938, attacked Jewish livelihood: now defined by religious affiliation and not Hungarian nationality, Jews saw their participation in civil services, institutes of higher learning and certain industries limited to 20 per cent of the total workforce. One year later, further restrictions on professional

---

1 Randolph L. Braham, *The Nazis' Last Victims: The Holocaust in Hungary* (Detroit: Wayne State University Press, 2002); and László Csősz, Gábor Kádár and Zoltán Vági, *The Holocaust in Hungary: Evolution of a Genocide* (Lanham, MD-Washington, DC: AltaMira Press-USHMM, 2013).

representation threatened to impoverish elements of the Jewish community. New legal interpretations — consistent with Nazi Germany's Nuremberg Race Laws — dictated that a "Jew" constituted any person with two Jewish grandparents. Some 100,000 Hungarian converts to Christianity — many of whom had converted to escape anti-Jewish persecution — now fell victim to the same restrictions as their Jewish brethren. A third antisemitic decree criminalized marriages between Jews and non-Jews in Hungary.

Despite her husband Sandor Nagy's Christianity, Bözsi's Jewishness deemed their only daughter, Éva, a "full Jew," later leaving both females vulnerable to the whims of the Arrow Cross leaders. Miraculously, the Nagy nuclear family remained unscathed throughout the Nazi occupation of Budapest.

If the first antisemitic decree rocked Hungary's Jews, the second decree devastated them. Under the guise of "cleansing" the army, the Miklós Horthy regime enacted two transformative pieces of legislation. The first designated Jews as "politically unreliable" and "unfit" to bear arms. The other piece of legislation pertained to the conscription of 100,000 Jewish men into forced labour battalions by 1942.

Jewish men spent the first two years performing relatively safe tasks, such as manual labour, mining, rail construction and general maintenance. However, by the time Bernat Löffler received his notification for conscription in early 1942, the situation for Jewish forced labourers had markedly deteriorated. Jewish men were required to wear an armband and civilian clothing, forbidden from carrying protective gear, and were subject to violent antisemitic attacks from non-Jewish soldiers and superiors. First to the fire, Jewish men received the most dangerous jobs, such as clearing minefields.

Bernat was temporarily released from service due to an ulcer, and briefly returned home to his wife and daughter. But such good fortune proved ephemeral. During a visit to see Bernat in the countryside where his unit was stationed, Susie recalled how her "haggard and worn" father predicted a journey deep inside the frozen fields of the Soviet Union. Between 25,000 and 40,000 Hungarian Jewish men, Bernat among them, died during their labour service.

With the widespread drafting of working-age men into forced labour, Hungarian Jewry was largely reduced to one of women, children and the elderly. Women like Zsuzsanna's mother and her aunt Malvin assumed head-of-household responsibilities. In addition to becoming the breadwinners, Jewish women shouldered the burden of making difficult decisions in hopes of surviving the war.

Although Hungarian Jewry experienced antisemitism, the community did not directly experience Nazi antisemitism until Germany invaded its former ally on March 19, 1944, in a concerted effort to keep Hungary on its side. The occupying leadership allowed Admiral Miklós Horthy to retain his post as Regent, but replaced Prime Minister Miklós Kállay with a pro-Nazi general, Döme Sztójay, who had previously served as Hungarian minister in Berlin. Sztójay directed the Hungarian military to continue fighting alongside the Axis powers, and agreed to assist in the roundup and deportation of Hungarian Jews. From May to early July 1944, nearly 440,000 Hungarian Jews were deported to the east; the majority were murdered upon arrival at the Auschwitz-Birkenau death camp, while a smaller number went to slave labour camps. When deportations ceased on July 7, 1944, the Jewish community in Budapest was the only one remaining in Hungary.

Hungary's pro-Nazi government promptly imposed a Jewish Council (*Judenrat*) in Budapest and executed a wave of new restrictions. "One after another, rules limiting our freedom were enacted; yellow star, Jewish houses, freedom of movement, deportation." Magda wore the yellow Star of David badge on her coat with pride, refusing to yield to the intended consequence of humiliation; in a futile attempt to financially sustain her family, Susie attempted (unsuccessfully) to sell the armbands for a small profit. Other measures designed to disenfranchise, impoverish, humiliate and control the city's Jews followed.

Three months after the German invasion, the Nazis decreed that Jews must move into "Jewish houses," designated buildings marked with a Star of David. More than 200,000 Jews came to reside in less than two thousand apartment buildings, leading to drastic reorganizations of living situations and crowded, unhygienic conditions. The Löfflers were permitted to remain in their apartment, though countless relatives were expelled from their homes. Strict curfews and access to public spaces, including parks and playgrounds, were particularly difficult for children. Susie recalled that her building's superintendent granted permission to "play ball in the courtyard" between designated curfew hours, an act of compassion in darkening times.

In October 1944, with the war seemingly in its last throes, a coup brought to power the fascist Arrow Cross Party, which was allied with the Nazis and committed to extending the war. Faced with the impending arrival of Soviet forces, the regime agreed to send 50,000 Jewish prisoners westward from Budapest to help fortify the German border in preparation for its inevitable breach. With no infrastructure in place to transport the prisoners, Arrow Cross officials forced their victims to march the 170-kilometre distance on foot over the course of eight days in convoys with few provisions. Spending the nights in the cold rain with no shelter, or in unsanitary stables or bombed factories, thousands died of starvation and exposure. Others were harassed by local bystanders and preyed upon by the Arrow Cross militiamen, who committed countless murders. Those who survived the march faced brutal and often lethal conditions as forced labourers and on further death marches that ensured their misery until liberation.[2]

---

2   László Csősz, *Death Blows Overhead: The Last Transports from Hungary, November 1944.* EHRI Blog post, 23 November 2017. Accessed: https://blog.ehri-project.eu/2017/11/23/hungary-1944/

Susie's mother, Magda, was one of some 70,000 deported Budapest Jews in November 1944. As Magda marched along the "highway of death" toward Austria, she somehow mailed postcards to her relatives in Budapest. While the censored postcards offered scant details about her specific circumstances, a November 19, 1944, note revealed Magda's suspicion that she and Susie would not be reunited:

My dear Zsuzsika. Your Mum is going far away and I don't know when we will meet again. My little child, think of your Mum often, because you are all I can think of and that is what sustains me. My flower, always be good, obedient, clean and tidy, take good care of your health. I really worry about my parents and my sister, but I hope you are all well. My dear Mum and Dad. May Heaven bless you as you deserve.

The death march deposited Magda in Lichtenwörth, a small Nazi camp in Austria. She remained in the camp until liberation on April 2, 1944. It wasn't until two decades after the war ended that Susan would discover the circumstances surrounding her mother's death.

As thousands of Jews were driven out of Budapest, the Hungarian leadership established an area to house the remaining Jews. The ghetto was sealed off from the rest of the city on December 10. The ghetto was divided into two sections: an "international ghetto" for recipients of protective papers by a neutral power; and a larger section for Jews without papers. In total, the ghetto held close to 70,000 Jews. Ghetto dwellers were vulnerable not only to starvation and disease, but also erratic Arrow Cross raids. Thousands of Jews were arbitrarily murdered on the banks of the Danube River.

Susan's aunt Malvin secured protective papers for her, her daughter and Susie to reside in a Red Cross home which offered the (temporary) guise of protection. This reprieve was short-lived. Arrow Cross soldiers liquidated their building, and the females were sent to the ghetto. Susie's time in the ghetto was equally short: "It was in darkness that I first beheld the walls of the ghetto," she wrote, and the following morning, she walked out of the unsealed prison. The guard on duty did not stop her.

Susie survived the balance of Nazi occupation and the Siege of Budapest (December 24, 1944, to February 12, 1945) within greater Budapest. She remained on the move, running from a Red Cross children's home to her uncle Sandor's sister's house; to the apartment of an aunt's Christian friends; to temporary hiding with non-Jewish acquaintances. Conditions in the region worsened, and supplies dwindled, in the final weeks of intense fighting. The Siege was one of the deadliest battles of World War II, resulting in the deaths of 38,000 civilians from bombings, starvation and the violent whims of Arrow Cross guards. Susie's memories of this period overwhelmingly speak to hunger and death: "What did it matter if I died from a bomb or from starvation?"

When the Soviets liberated the city on February 13, 1945, 100,000 Jews remained in the ghetto. Miraculously, nearly all of Susie's maternal relatives survived the Shoah. Susie spent the months after liberation recuperating at a Zionist children's home in Debrecen, and restarted her studies. Upon returning to Budapest, Susie took up residence in an apartment bursting at the seams with family. With the love of her now-impoverished and suffering relatives aside, Susie's post-war life in Budapest was lonely and painful. In an effort to change her circumstances and paint a brighter future for herself, the teenager took a leap of faith and made her next move — to Canada.

In August of 1948, following a two-week journey across the Atlantic Ocean, Susie Löffler disembarked at Pier 21 in Halifax, Nova Scotia. Susie and her shipmates entered Canada via the War Orphans Project (WOP), a refugee resettlement scheme sponsored by the Canadian Jewish Congress (CJC). Planning for the rescue mission initially began with the outbreak of war. In October 1942, pursuant to Order-in-Council 1647, Immigration Director Frederick Charles Blair granted permission for 500 Jewish children to enter Canada through Vichy France. The Allies' 1942 invasion of Vichy North Africa caused the mission to be aborted. None of the children slated for rescue to Canada survived the war.[3]

Nearly five years later, in April 1947, Parliament re-tabled and moved the War Orphan Project (WOP) bill, authorizing the immediate distribution of one thousand visas to Jewish orphans up to eighteen years of age. After undergoing intensive physical and psychological examinations and establishing proof of age and "orphan" status, 1,123 Jewish war orphans entered Canada between September 1947 and March 1952. Many, like Susie, had borne witness to incomprehensible horrors. All sought a new beginning far from the devastation of post-war Europe.[4]

The American Jewish Joint Distribution Committee (JDC), assuming the role and responsibilities of the project's accredited overseas agent on behalf of the Canadian Jewish Congress, eagerly endorsed the project.[5] Further, the JDC garnered preferential treatment

---

3   Irving Abella and Harold Troper, *None is Too Many: Canada and the Jews of Europe 1933–1948* (Toronto: Lester & Orpen Dennys Publishers, 1982), 111–117.

4   Ben Lappin, *The Redeemed Children: The Story of the Rescue of War Orphans by the Jewish Community of Canada* (Toronto: University of Toronto Press, 1963); Adara Goldberg, *Holocaust Survivors in Canada: Exclusion, Inclusion, Transformation, 1947–1955* (Winnipeg: University of Manitoba Press, 2015); Fraidie Martz, *Open Your Hearts: The Story of the Jewish War Orphans in Canada* (Don Mills: Véhicule Press, 1996); and *Open Hearts – Closed Doors: The War Orphans Project*, an online exhibit from the Vancouver Holocaust Education Centre, hosted by Virtual Museum Canada: http://www.virtualmuseum.ca/sgc-cms/expositions-exhibitions/orphelins-orphans/english/

5   Founded in 1914, the American Jewish Joint Distribution Committee, also known as the Joint, is the leading Jewish humanitarian aid organization, serving communities in more than seventy countries around the world. After World War II, the Joint provided financial aid to surviving Jewish communities, and attended to

to the wop over other children survivors' emigration schemes to Australia, South Africa and the United States, based on three highly desirable features: 1) institutionalization of the young survivors would not form any part of the plan; 2) local child welfare agencies would provide 'periodic supervision' of children and foster homes; and 3) placements would be in foster homes approved by local social and child welfare agencies, with ultimate adoption as the goal.[6]

These conditions attracted the attention of impoverished adult guardians of war orphans, who were themselves recovering from the Shoah. Fearing an uncertain future for her young charge in a postwar Hungary that had been incorporated into the Soviet-Communist zone of influence, and satisfied that the cjc would fulfill its commitment to guarantee adoption, Susie's Aunt Malvin agreed to register her niece for the War Orphans Project. And so it was that Susie was sent away from her beloved grandparents, aunts, uncles and cousins, to face alone an unknown future in a faraway country.

Susie's new life in Canada hit an immediate sour note upon her placement in Vegreville, Alberta. This rural farming community, some 100 kilometres from Edmonton, boasted a total of six Jewish families but no Jewish teenage girls, or Hungarian speakers of any faith. This included the Kleins, the middle-aged couple planning to adopt Susie.

In a diary entry dated November 24, 1948, Susie — now known by the anglicized Susan — proclaimed:

---

the daily needs of refugees in post-war Europe.

6 Letter from Moses W. Beckleman to All Country and Field Directors, Subject: Orphan Children Immigration to Canada, 2 July 1947, Paris, 1-2, 1945–1954 New York Collection – Folder: Canada, Immigration of Children, 1946–1950, ajdc Archives, Jerusalem, Israel. One marked exception to the "no institutionalization" plan was the installation of short-term centres to receive and process new arrivals.

How I hate to be here! How I hate everybody! Did I give up my life at home to come here? I wanted change, adventure, and I am here in this awfulness. I want so much to do something, to be somebody, to travel, to see different things, to live a colourful life. But I must stay here. Should I spend my whole life here?... I cannot imagine living such a vacant, barren life as most people seem to: live, work, struggle, marry. Some may succeed in acquiring certain things, yet are grinding up their youth doing it. I don't want such a life, I don't.

Superficially, Susan's conditions were relatively good. She had been placed in a private home with foster parents who genuinely cared about her well-being. Susan tried to settle into her new environs and build a life for herself in what she described as "cow country." But, beneath the surface, the situation was far from idyllic: "It's strange and exasperating that I have no friends and no hope for any." Although the Kleins treated her kindly and with genuine affection, Susan could not envision a future for herself in a place that lacked social, educational and meaningful opportunities to build a family of her own.

Unbeknownst to Susan or her family, plans for adoption as the "end goal" of the War Orphans Project had been summarily abandoned by the Canadian Jewish Congress long before she even arrived in Vegreville. The original plan was modified to replace regulated foster care-cum-adoption with "suitable paid living quarters" for the youth. This constituted a significant and substantive shift in the parameters of the resettlement directive. Adoption, the promise made to European guardians and the orphans themselves, was no longer the project's endgame. The coordinating bodies concluded that most of the orphans were "too old," and therefore not desirable candidates for adoption. Others, like Susan — upon realizing that the Kleins expected her to forgo her secondary school studies and attend a technical college — rejected the conditions surrounding the proposed adoption, preferring to strike out on her own.[7]

Susan presented her case to the Canadian Jewish Congress: she wished to move to Toronto. She understood that the possibility of a "free" home upon transfer would be slim, and that financial aid would not be proffered. Susan agreed to the terms. But the transfer to Toronto never transpired; instead, she was resettled in Winnipeg. There, Susan would face many more hardships before achieving her educational goals.

Too Many Goodbyes tells the story of one young girl whose destiny was not what she had imagined as a little girl. But it was the life she was given. Taking heed of her parents' guiding hands, Susan Garfield asserted her independence in the wake of tragedy, challenged imposed limitations to her personal growth, and built a home and family of her own. Her resilience to trauma is demonstrative of the human spirit, and a model by which to live our own lives.

Dr. Adara Goldberg
Director, Holocaust Resource Center
Kean University
2019

---

7   In the end, the War Orphans Project produced fewer than one hundred formal adoptions, although in a number of cases strong informal relationships did evolve between orphans and foster families.

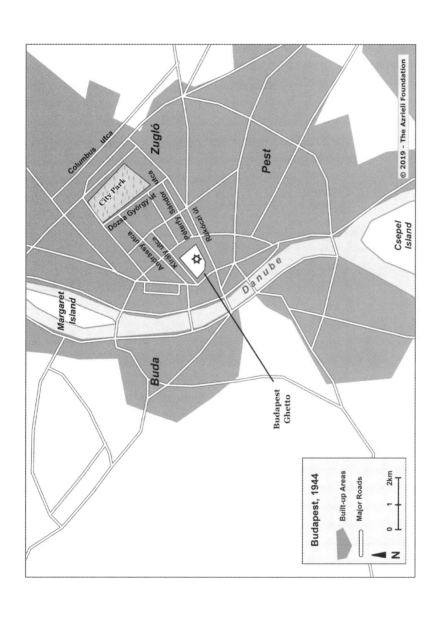

Budapest, 1944

Built-up Areas

Major Roads

0   1   2km

N

Margaret Island

Buda

City Park

Columbus utca

Zugló

Andrássy utca

Dózsa György út

Király utca

Pest

Péterfy Sándor utca

Rákóczi út

Danube

Csepel Island

Budapest Ghetto

Susan Garfield Family Tree

MATERNAL GREAT-GRANDPARENTS:
Regina m. *Herman Lieber*

GREAT AUNT:
Giza m. *Miklos Irsai*
- *Erno*
- *George*
- *Mimi* m. *Istvan Koves* —— *Peter*

GREAT AUNT:
Szeren m. *Herschkowitz (last name)*
- *Alfred* m. *Ági* —— *Anat*
- *Laszlo (Laci)*

GREAT UNCLE:
Pal m. *Melanie* ———— *Helga* m. *Willie Velloso*

MATERNAL GRANDPARENTS:
Eszter Lieber m. *Farkas Weisz*

MOTHER:
Magdolna (Magdus) Weisz m. ————————————

AUNT:
Ilus m. *Osztermann (last name)* —— *Andor (Bandi)* m. *Edith* —— *Susan*

AUNT:
Malvin m. *Géza Pollak* —— *Ágnes (Ági)* m. *Frici (Fred)*
- *Kathy*
- *George*

AUNT:
Elizabeth (Bözsi) m. *Sandor Nagy* ———— *Éva* m. *Frank*
- *Andrea*
- *Ronald*

UNCLE:
Lajos m. *Magda* ———— *Marietta (Marika)*

AUNT:
Ibolya (Ibi) m. *Pista Rona* ————
- *Robi*
- *Kati*
- *Tunde*

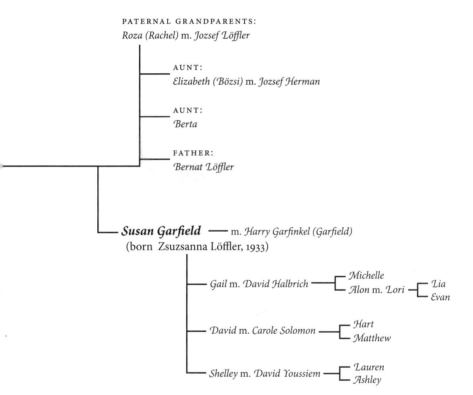

PATERNAL GRANDPARENTS:
Roza (Rachel) m. *Jozsef Löffler*

AUNT:
Elizabeth (Bözsi) m. *Jozsef Herman*

AUNT:
Berta

FATHER:
Bernat Löffler

Susan Garfield —— m. *Harry Garfinkel (Garfield)*
(born Zsuzsanna Löffler, 1933)

Gail m. *David Halbrich* ——⌐ *Michelle*
                              ⌐ *Alon* m. *Lori* ——⌐ *Lia*
                                                            Evan

David m. *Carole Solomon* ——⌐ *Hart*
                                     Matthew

Shelley m. *David Youssiem* ——⌐ *Lauren*
                                     Ashley

To my beautiful, vital, young and wonderful parents, who died alone, without ever knowing what happened to me and to the rest of their family; whom I never stopped missing and longing for; and who loved me unconditionally and more.

I also dedicate this memoir to my descendants, for whom I wanted to write down what happened to me and to my family.

I am neither infant nor happy grandfather
Nor parent, nor lover
Of anyone, of anyone.
I am, as every man is, Majesty,
The North Pole, the Secret, the Stranger,
The will-o'-the-wisp in the distance, the will-o'-the-wisp in the distance.

But alas! I cannot remain this way.
I should like to show myself to the world,
So that someone sees me, so that someone sees me.

This is why I sing and I torment myself.
I should love to be loved.
I wish to be of someone, I wish to be of someone.

"I Should Love to Be Loved," Endre Ady
Translation by Eli Siegel (*Hail, American Development*, New York:
    Definition Press, 1968)

Part One: Diary

2.

Bevezetés. Tulajdonképpen azért írok
naplót, hogy majd sok-sok év múlva, mikor majd ezer ránc szántja sima arc-
bőröm megmutathassok gyermekeimnek,
unokáimnak. Beleírom a sok küzdelmes, ha-
bonás életet, a fejenőlást és még sok más
szívfájdító dolgot. Most én mutatkozom be.

Holnap leszek 11 éves. Őszintén beval-
lom, nagyon tetszem magamnak. Alul egész
szőke még a hajam, felül már barnás.
Mikor kisebb voltam nagynéném (Irének
hívják) esküvőjén fehér ruhába voltam.
Mikor fényképeztek 1½ éve előtt álltam lehaj-
tott fejjel. Alig lehetett látni, mert a
nagynéném fehér menyasszonyi ruha volt
és az én fejem is olyan volt, mint a ruha
Úgy látszik mindig eltérek a tárgytól,
de azért folytatom leírásomat. Homlokom
középnagy. Szemöldököm vastag, barna, de nem formátlan. Nagy kék szemem
van. Felső szempillám barna az alsó szőke
és mind a kettő hosszú. Szájad szép. Or-
rom nagyon formás és pisze. (Nekem a
pisze orr nagyon tetszik.) Szám barnás,

The first page of Susan's diary. June 2, 1944.

1944

June 2, 1944

The reason I'm writing a diary is so that many, many years from now, when my smooth face will be furrowed by a thousand wrinkles, I will be able to show it to my children and grandchildren. I will write about the many hard struggles of life during the war, the occupation and many other heart-wrenching things. Now it's time for me to introduce myself.

I'm going to be eleven years old tomorrow. I can honestly say that I'm very fond of my looks. My hair is still completely blonde at the bottom, and somewhat brownish at the top. When I was younger, I wore a white dress at my aunt's wedding (her name is Ibi). When they were taking the pictures, I was standing in front of Ibi with my head slightly bowed. You could hardly see me, because my aunt wore a white wedding dress and my head was the colour of her gown. It seems I have strayed from the subject, but I will get back to describing myself. My forehead is average height. My eyebrows are thick and brown, but not shapeless. I have big blue eyes, my upper eyelashes are dark but the lower ones are fair, and they are all long. In other words, pretty. My nose is very shapely and turned up. (I really like turned-up noses.) My mouth is a nice shape and rather small. My chin is pointed, which is prettier than a round chin. My face is oval. I am a young girl of medium height, and somewhat on the skinny side. I'm going to have a good figure; my ankles are slender already. By the way, my name is Zsuzsanna Veronika Löffler, but at home everyone calls me Zsuzsi [Susie].

I have just finished the first year of public school, and what I want more than anything is to be accepted into the gimnázium.[1] *I don't have much of a chance because I had a low mark in Hungarian, despite the fact that my essays were graded excellent for grammar and excellent for composition, with a low mark only for penmanship. It only happened once that I had a low mark for grammar. My marks for the oral portion were not bad either. I think that the Hungarian teacher has it in for me.*

The war is in its sixth year. I was five when it started.[2] All I can remember is war, war. The Germans are now occupying Hungary, and it is very bad for the Jews. These days we often have to hide in the cellar from Russian, American or English bombs. At night we even have to leave our nice soft beds and head for the cellar.

My father has been conscripted into the Labour Service, and it's more than a year since he disappeared on the Russian front.

Now I'm ready to start my diary.

June 3

Mother promised to buy me a board game. I asked for a Monopoly set. She promised to buy it in the morning. My aunt Malvin is having lunch with us because my cousin Ági is working and does not come home for lunch. Her father, Uncle Géza, has been conscripted, and Malvin sees no point in cooking just for herself. She arrived at 11:15, so we could only go and get Monopoly after lunch. Mother took forever to get dressed, and I was very impatient, and finally we left. Once we'd bought the set, I rushed home because I had organized a party for my eleventh birthday, to which I invited seven girls. I will give their names here: Ági and Mari Székely; Mari and I went to elementary school together, but she is attending gimnázium *now. Ági is her little sister. As well, I invited*

---

1   Susan would have just finished the equivalent of Grade 5 in Canada. The *gimnázium* was the high school for ten- to eighteen-year-olds.

2   Susan was born on June 3, 1933. In September 1939, at the start of World War II, she was six years old.

Judit Haar, whom I will refer to as Jutka in my diary. The reason I'm mentioning this is because there is another girl called Judit Róth. She is Judit. I don't want to mix up the two. I also invited Zsuzsi Löwy, who is a neighbour of ours. She is already fourteen but is very short. I'm taller than she is. I invited Maja Neugewurtz, who I know because when we were born our mothers were in the same hospital and we were born the same day. It's her birthday today, too. I also asked Marika Weisz, my six-year-old cousin. Jutka didn't show up. I don't know why, but I'm really going to give her a piece of my mind. Except for Judit and Zsuzsi they all arrived late. I was very anxious. Maja only arrived when we had already finished our afternoon treat and had started the raffle. Then the parents came to pick up their kids. Maja stayed until 9:00 [p.m.]. I walked her home and went inside. I browsed through her books and wrote in her autograph book.

The Jews have to wear a star, a ten-centimetre-wide yellow star in the shape of a Star of David. Maja has some for sale. I took a few to sell. She charges 150 pengős each and I will charge 170. I got home at 9:45. Mother was already in bed. She was very angry at me. I will pacify her later.

June 4

I was still in bed when Father's sister Berta arrived with a [birthday] gift. Then came my aunts Ibi and Malvin. I got up because I was supposed to take some stamps over to Ibi's husband. I got dressed and went over to the Löwys' and the Schnellers' [neighbours in the building, to find out if they were interested in buying some stars]. *Klári, a twenty-year-old girl, asked me to bring over my presents to show her. I took over the Monopoly game, and Robi, Klári's brother (seventeen years old), asked me to play a game later on. I played Monopoly with Zsuzsi Löwy, but I soon grew tired of it. Zsuzsi went over to the Schnellers' and asked if they'd like to play. They were busy. There's a sweet little two-year-old boy on the second floor, Robika. Zsuzsi brought him upstairs to play with him, but I preferred to read. Then we had lunch. Then I read some more. Afterwards I went over to the Schnellers' to find out what was up. They asked me to bring over the game. We played for a while.*

Later, Mother called me home, saying it was time to go to Ibi's place. I didn't want to. I sat down on the floor and grabbed hold of the carpet with all my might. Mother was arguing with me. Finally I got up and sat down on the sofa. I was talking back to her. Mother finally picked up one of my shoes (the same shoes I refused to put on because I didn't feel like going), and she hit me on the knee with it. It hurt something awful. Mother said that she was going to get washed and I should put on my shoes in the meantime. Just to show her, I took a long time to lace them up so that she had finished her bath by the time I did up my laces. At the last minute I decided I was hungry. At last my belly was full and we set off. On the tram I was worried if I'd be able to get a children's ticket. I was. There was a woman standing across from us. She had no breasts to speak of. Ibi and her husband were not at home because they were in the shop. We went over because Ibi wanted to celebrate their wedding anniversary, which was today. In the end, nothing came of it because Uncle Pista [Ibi's husband] *has to report for Labour Service tomorrow morning and they need to pack and say their goodbyes. So we made a trip for nothing.*

When I got home, I met Maja on the staircase. She was coming from our place. We played with my dolls and had a game of Monopoly. She left at 7:00. Then I brought Robika upstairs to play with him. Then Zsuzsi Löwy came home from her aunt's. We played Monopoly until 10:00 p.m. It is 10:30 now, and the air-raid warning has just sounded. I have no idea what's going to happen. The last we heard on the radio was that there were bombers flying over Bácska, Baja and Szeged.[3]

---

3 A region and cities that are between two hundred and three hundred kilometres from Budapest, where Susan lived.

June 9

Don't be cross with me, my dear diary, because I haven't written for so long, but no interesting events have taken place recently. But today something happened at my next-door neighbours, the Löwys'. Luci, Zsuzsi's sister, is a nasty, heartless girl. She keeps calling her mother all sorts of names. Well, Bandi Gotteszmann, Luci's fiancé, who is in the Labour Service, has disappeared on the Russian front. Bandi's best friend, Lajos [Lali] Weissmann, asked Luci to marry him. In Hungarian, Gotteszmann means "God man." Weissmann means "White man."[4]

June 10

Luci's fiancé arrived with a big bouquet of flowers. The Löwys were not at home. He left the flowers with a neighbour.

In the afternoon, Mother and I were over at Auntie Schneller's,[5] who told us that Luci doesn't want to marry Lajos because he doesn't know how to dance. There must be something wrong with her brains. Zsuzsi slept over at my place. There was an air raid. We couldn't sleep. We got up, played Monopoly, and drank some liqueur.[6] It must have been two in the morning by the time we went to sleep.

June 11

Zsuzsi told the Schnellers what we had been up to the previous night. Ila Schneller, in turn, repeated the story to Mother. We didn't get in trouble for it.

---

4 Susan actually means in Yiddish or in German, not in Hungarian.

5 Auntie Schneller is not a biological relation. In Hungarian the word *néni* (aunt/ auntie) is often used as a term of respect or affection for an older person; *bácsi* (uncle) is the male equivalent.

6 Susan's mother was not at home during this incident because she was acting as a warden for the building, which was common for civilians to do at that point in the war. Susan and her friend found the liqueur in a bag that had been prepared in case of an air raid.

June 13

The Löwys' relatives showed up next door because their houses had been bombed. A lady weighing at least 120 kilos and her very pretty little girl. Truth be told, an eighteen-year-old is no longer a little girl, but it makes no difference to me. She is very nice. Her name is Ibi. Her mother is called Auntie Annus. She is also very nice.

June 16

Jewish houses are being set up.[7] Thank God we can stay in our building. I do not know who is going to come here to live with us. I went to see the Rónas, but they had already found a place to move to. Grandmother's family is staying put as well. But not my aunt Malvin. She and her family will come either to Grandmother's place or to our place. They have until the 21st to move.

June 17

Mother and I were having a leisurely supper at 6:00 p.m. when we heard a blood-curdling scream. Had Auntie Löwy [Zsuzsi's mother] committed suicide? All the blood rushed to my head. I dashed out. Auntie Löwy had run over to the Weiszes'. She was not feeling well. I am going to recount, step by step, what happened. Luci Löwy is walking down the street. A guy comes up to her and tells her to remove her yellow star and go see a movie with him. Of course, Luci was not willing to do that. She went to visit a friend of hers. The guy who had stopped her was wearing a soldier's uniform. By the time Luci finished her visit, the guy was waiting for her in civilian clothes. He asked her to be his girlfriend. Luci told him to forget it, that she was getting married in two days' time. Then he offered to marry her. Of course that's not possible because the guy is a Christian. Finally they arrived at our building. The guy insisted

---

7 Designated buildings that Jews were forced to move into three months after the Nazis occupied Hungary. See the glossary for more information.

on coming upstairs. They met Luci's fiancé, Lali, on the staircase. He and Luci rushed ahead and slammed the door in the guy's face. Then he knocked on the door and Auntie Löwy opened it. He told her he was a detective. He lied to her, saying that Luci had removed the star and gone to a movie. What a rotten liar. That's when Auntie Löwy rushed out and started to feel unwell. They [the police] *caught the guy, and since Luci didn't have any identity papers because they'd been submitted to the marriage registry office, they* [the police] *took her away. She came back within half an hour. An exceptionally nice policeman came by in the evening to calm down the distressed family.*

June 18
Auntie Szidi [Zsuzsi Löwy's aunt] *was here and she said that Zsuzsi was going to her grandfather's and that she'd found an apartment. Which is to say that a few buildings were designated as Jewish houses and all the Jews were supposed to move into them. At least six people are supposed to share one room. No one will have their own apartment. Thank heavens our building was one of the designated ones. Auntie Szidi's husband is sick and Auntie Löwy doesn't want to take him in. Auntie Löwy thought that* [Auntie Szidi] *was lying just so that her husband would be accepted. Auntie Szidi is a Christian. In the evening, Zsuzsi and I asked if it was true that they had found another apartment.*

June 19
Today would have been the day when Luci and Lali got married but the wedding didn't take place. Lali went to the police station and they told him not to get married because the guy [who had harassed Luci] *could carry on with his accusations and then Lali would be picked up and sent to an internment camp, and if they didn't find him at home, they could take his wife instead. Luci cried all day long, even though she doesn't love Lali.*

June 20
Lali sent some flowers and spent the evening at Luci's.

June 21
Two people have moved in [to our apartment] *already, a mother and her daughter.*

June 22
Tomorrow, in the afternoon, I'm going with the Székelys to visit a relative of theirs. They have a home with a garden that's going to be taken away. Let us enjoy it while we can. They [Mari and Ági] *were here this afternoon and we had fun playing. When they left, I brought up Robika, a beautiful sweet little two-year-old boy. After I took him back, I started writing in my diary, and now I'm going to bed.*

P.S. Mother's cousin [Mimi Koves] *is going to move in here with her son, Peter, who is eight years old. I'm not happy about it because he is a brat and doesn't let me read.*

June 23
I spent the day in Bethesda Street [with the Székelys]. *First we* [Ági and Mari] *went to the cellar because that's where they kept the toys. When we came upstairs, we played for a while. Afterwards Ági and Mari were called down to the cellar. I wanted to go too, but I was told to stay put. My heart ached terribly and I decided never to visit them again. I thought they were going to get a present and that's why they didn't want me there. They got some clothes. Then I got a lot of books* [from them]. *They were right to keep the nice stuff for themselves but it still hurt my feelings. Afterwards we had a good time playing. The three of us formed a league for good manners. Whoever can write a lot of good rules for it by tomorrow will be the leader. I will go there tomorrow after all.*

June 24

Peter [Koves] *and his mother arrived. We had already given up on them. It was after 10:00* [p.m.] *when they showed up.*

June 25

We are only allowed to be out on the street between 2:00 and 5:00 p.m.

June 26

Peti [Peter] *keeps hitting me and I hit him back. (Naturally.) In the end I am always the one who gets told off, even though I am the one who is in the right.*

June 26

Thank God. We are allowed to be out on the street from 11:00 to 5:00 as of today.

June 27

As we are not allowed to go to the park or to the playground, the super-intendent gave us permission to play ball in the courtyard between 5:00 and 6:00 p.m. That is really nice of him.

June 28

Peti is completely out of control. He has become terribly saucy.

June 29

I play Monopoly every night with Ilonka Weisz.

June 30

I started playing ball with the other kids. Pali is the referee.

July 1
These days we spend a lot of time in the cellar [because of the constant air raids]. *The air is so bad you feel like you're suffocating.*

July 2
This morning the air-raid sirens sounded again. They don't even let you have your breakfast in peace.

July 3
I couldn't fall asleep until midnight. The adults were whispering until 11:00 p.m. When they finally stopped, Peti called out, "You can't sleep with Grandma around, she snores so much!" Then there was an air raid. Bombers over Budapest. Then I get up and they [the adults] *are having a loud argument.*

October 3
I haven't written for ages, my dear diary, but I will make up for it. I am going to make up for what I missed. But now inspiration has struck and I'm going to write short stories for young people. We are nearing the end of the war. The Russians have reached Szeged.[8] *I have already finished a short story. It's passable.*

October 10
We are living through very important times. I will take you step by step through the happenings of the last few days. Three days ago, Mom and I went to my school to find out if I would be admitted to the gimnázium. *They told us to apply on the 12th. From there I went to my* [paternal] *grandma's place on Király Street. Mother accompanied me. We met an acquaintance. He told us that Jews should avoid walking in front of a*

---

8   During the Battle of Debrecen, the Soviets reached Szeged around October 11.

certain building. German soldiers are stationed in that building. I went to see Grandma. [Aunt] *Bözsi said that the Hungarians had asked* [the Soviets] *for an armistice and they were granted it, but they don't dare to announce it publicly yet because of the Germans. (That would be great, I thought.) Afterwards I went to Malvin's for lunch.* [Cousin] *Éva was there. I had promised to go and see her on Tuesday. Today is Tuesday.*

November 2

I am going to write down everything that happened last month. I was on my way home from Malvin's after lunch. In front of our house Pötyi [Wilhelm] *was rocking her tiny niece Zsuzsi to sleep. Pötyi told me that* [her cousin] *Évi* [Fohn] *had just gone upstairs to have lunch and that she was feeling bored. She asked me to stay with her and entertain her. We had barely exchanged a few words when Évi came bursting out of the door like a whirlwind.*

— What has happened? What's going on? we demanded to know.

— There was just an announcement on the radio that the Hungarians have made an armistice with the Russians.[9]

We went wild with joy. Like prisoners who'd been sentenced to death but whose sentence was overturned and who were let out of prison and given back their freedom. Then Évi warned us that we had better go upstairs because there was bound to be a commotion [following the announcement].

And was there ever a commotion! Dear God, what have we Jews done to you that you punish us so? The star was taken down from the entrance of our building, then the superintendent gave it such a big kick that the glass broke. Many people have already removed the yellow star from all their clothing. I have been very happy before in my life, but never as happy as now.

---

9   The radio announcement Susan refers to was on October 15.

But then Horthy [Miklós Horthy, Regent of Hungary] *gave a speech. I am going to give* [just a bit of] *its content here: "Hitler summoned me to Berlin, and while I was there, they* [the German army] *occupied Hungary. The German soldiers looted and plundered the whole of Hungary."*[10]

---

10 Susan, who was still only eleven when she wrote these words, is perhaps conflating two different events and is not quite correct here: At the time of this announcement, Horthy was in Budapest, Hungary. As Horthy was attempting to extricate Hungary from the war, the Nazis kidnapped his son, forcing Horthy to support a coup by the extremist and antisemitic Hungarian Arrow Cross Party. (See the glossary for more information on the Arrow Cross Party). It was in fact several months earlier, on March 18, 1944, that Hitler had summoned Horthy — to Schloss Klessheim, a palace near Salzburg, not Berlin — after which the German occupation of Hungary occurred.

1947

January

Each time I happen upon this diary I seriously contemplate tearing it or burning it, for I find it embarrassing to read, even to myself. On second thought, though, I give it reprieve because I believe it's the truth; that's the way I was and I described my true feelings. What's more, I end up adding to it.

I won't even try to write down how much has happened since the last time I wrote. Such things can never, ever be forgotten anyway. I have come across this notebook by pure chance. God only knows where it has been hiding all these years, and the reason for its surfacing now, I have no idea. It is tough to read my old diary, the diary of an eleven-year-old girl. It's almost incredible how conceited I used to be back then. But I am not anymore. I have changed some since I described myself. My hair is darker, my face rounder. Now I am chubby rather than slender. That's all. People consider me pretty. Yes, pretty. But I have changed tremendously since the time I wrote the diary.

The gap that exists in time is best left unfilled, as it contains neither joy nor beauty, but death, fear of death and fathomless pain. My dear Father, my dear Mother, you are no more. No one on earth will ever know my feelings about this. I may appear callous to others. I once overheard a relative tell my mother, "This child never mentions her father;

she probably never thinks of him." Now it is the same with both [parents]. *But I don't care what people think. I hate, abhor, despise people. I may be wicked but it is their fault. I didn't want not to care. I became selfish, an egotist. Only "I" exists for me. Nothing else exists, nothing I care about.*

I will probably be leaving for Canada sometime soon. I will be adopted through the Joint.[11] *I thought I would write a short autobiography on the remaining pages of this exercise book and in the framework of this diary.*

I was an only child and I was spoiled as only children often are. Though we were not rich, I was never in need of anything. The first years of my life were spent uneventfully and probably very happily. I will not write a detailed account about that period, as my memory doesn't stretch that far back.

In the first years of my schooling, I was an indifferent student. Many days my father sat patiently with me to help me master the three Rs [reading, writing and arithmetic]. *My teacher maintained that I had the ability to be an A student, which did not particularly flatter me for I believed this claim was made about all students, including the stupid ones.*

I did perfect my reading ability very quickly and it became my favourite pastime. I would forgo all other activities in favour of a good book. My father wanted me to become a doctor and this sounded like a good idea to me. In order to reach this goal, I would have to go to the gimnázium. *But these things were still far away. At the moment, war was in progress, though I was aware of it only dimly. The time came, however, when it introduced its ugly head. My father was called up to enter the slave labour force. My mother and I saw him off at the railway station. Many of the women were crying. I was holding my parents' hands and watched uncomprehendingly. I also noticed jeering smiles*

---

11 The American Jewish Joint Distribution Committee.

on the faces of many onlookers. My eight-year-old soul revolted against this exhibition. Whatever the reason is for your crying, don't do it in front of others. Don't expose your pain to the malicious gloating of unsympathetic strangers.

At that time my father was released because of an ulcer condition. He returned home at dawn and I snuggled into bed with my parents while my father recounted his experiences. Another draft notice arrived in December of 1942. This time we had permission to visit him in the countryside, where he was stationed. My mother and I took the train. It was in the dead of winter; we walked for a long time in the snow and cold. He looked haggard and worn. He said, "Why didn't you bring my mother? God knows if I will ever see her again."

My mother carried on my father's business. The rare air raid was all that brought the war closer to us. Just before a geography test we kids even prayed for one.

My friends and I decided to raise some money to help the Jewish Aid Association. It was my idea to put on a play. A friend's mother agreed to let us use her house and also to be the director of our play. The play was to take place on a Sunday afternoon, March 19 [1944]. We were all very excited about it. In the morning we had our final rehearsal. As we were leaving for home, we ran into [Ágnes's] sister, who seemed very agitated and said that we must hurry home. We took the streetcar for a comparatively short ride home, and as we got off, she whispered, "The Germans are here." My thoughts were galloping in my brain with lightning speed, then stopped at one, from which there was no escape. It set on my brain, its weight crushing my skull with terrible force: The Germans are killing Jews. My eyes started tearing and I suddenly found myself running home. The news would not be believed. But soon enough it was confirmed. One after another, rules limiting our freedom were enacted; yellow star, Jewish houses, freedom of movement, deportation. Everyone from the countryside was deported. We lived in constant fear. Then, on October 15, Horthy requested a truce from the Russians. The joy that greeted this announcement is indescribable. It didn't last long.

By the same evening, the Arrow Cross had taken control of the radio station and what was left of Hungary. The news filtering to us was stupefying. Groups of people carrying hand luggage were marching on the street. Where could they be taken? When will our turn come?

At night we went to bed with all our clothes on, falling into a restless sleep, listening for the ring. When it happened, we ran into the hall, terrified. Arrow Cross men accompanied by police entered the building and ordered all men between the ages of sixteen and fifty and women between ages of sixteen and forty to quickly pack and be ready to leave.

At the first opportunity I had, I went to stay with my aunt Malvin. The ghetto was being set up now. My aunt obtained Red Cross papers for my cousin and myself. I won't even try to describe conditions there [in the Red Cross house]. *Hordes of people; throngs pressing on top of each other. Yet more and more people filed in, with or without papers. We slept on benches, as tight as sardines. Just as bunk beds were being built for more comfort, the Arrow Cross men arrived. Pack, sort people out, line up, march. It was in darkness that I first beheld the walls of the ghetto. So this will be our prison or our vault. We were taken into one apartment along with twenty-five other people. At the time the ghetto was not yet sealed off. I simply walked out the following day. The guard did not stop me.*

Now I went to a Red Cross home for children. I was "little mother" to several younger children. Awful conditions, lice and scabies. My aunt who was married to a Christian came to visit one day and brought a postcard that she received from my mother. Then, the day they [the Arrow Cross] *came for us, I escaped through the basement window.*

My uncle took me to hide with his sister in the countryside. I was miserable. I had lice, which I was ashamed to tell them. I insisted on going back to Budapest. I took a morning train on Christmas Day. This train turned out to be the last one to leave. By the same afternoon, the Russians occupied that village.

I went to live with another aunt who was hiding with Christian friends. We had practically no food. I stood in line for a whole morn-

ing for a small piece of bread, with bullets flying overhead and planes dropping bombs. Dead bodies were lying everywhere. Some were killed by bombs, some by flying matter or from air pressure; others were killed by Germans. Those ones had posters with different descriptions hanging around their necks. "This is what happens to hiding Jews." Or "This is what happens to those who stay out after five o'clock." Now the curfew applied to everyone. In the beginning I would cross the street horrified when I saw a dead body. Then I got used to it. Once I even forced myself to look at one's face. This fills me with horror even at the distance of three years. Dead horses were lying on the roads and people came with knives, carving pieces from it.

When we had no food left, I declared that I would go and get some. What did it matter if I died from a bomb or from starvation? I set out walking, but after a while the noise of the shooting became deafening and too frightening, even for me. I saw an Arrow Cross man and I decided to ask him if it was possible to go to Zugló [on the outskirts of Budapest]. I thought that if I dared approach him, he would not suspect me of being a Jew. He said, "Little girl, you better go home. The Russians have taken Zugló." I was perhaps fifteen minutes walking distance from there. I stood for quite a while in front of the building my aunt used to live in and where she had some gentile friends, undecided. Dare I risk going in, where many could recognize me? I finally did. They fed me until I was full and made me sleep there. They told me that another aunt had taken some food supplies from them; they also gave me her address. Now I went off to see this aunt. She and her husband were hiding in a basement shop with the owners of the place, with false papers. They would not allow me to leave. First of all, my aunt doused my head with petroleum because I was crawling with lice. Everyone was walking around sniffing and wondering where the smell came from. I just about died of embarrassment.

Finally, liberation. We pinched our arms and rubbed our eyes and asked ourselves incredulously, Are we dreaming or is this reality? We were given our lives and human dignity.

Still there was no food in the city. A Zionist organization, with the assistance of the Joint, was taking children to Debrecen. I decided to go also. I stayed there for four months; while there, I ate and ate. I was insatiable. The person who had to be distracted by a story to force a meal on, who was nicknamed Susie Thread, practically rolled home from Debrecen.

While I was busy eating in Debrecen, my peers were going to school to make up for the lost year. I, too, started studying, when I came down with hepatitis. I recovered two weeks before the next school session was to start. With a private tutor I studied day and night and succeeded in writing the required exams for honours. In the third grade of public school I received all As. The following summer I studied for special exams in order to be able to transfer to the gimnázium, *where I continued being an A student. I earned pocket money by tutoring.*

Why do I want to go to Canada? Only sad memories bind me to Hungary. It will be painful to leave my relatives, aunts, grandparents and cousins who love me and who don't dare detain me for fear of reproach in the future. My utmost desire is to leave, and I would consider myself unfortunate if I would not be successful in this. I do not wish to live in a place where everything I see awakens memories and tears at healing wounds. Here everything drags me backwards — the past, the people. Only in a new environment, far from here, can I look forward to the future.

1948-1949

Vegreville, Alberta[12]

October 9, 1948

I was finally on my way. The train was rushing toward Paris. To see Paris and die. Well, having seen it, I won't go along with this statement. Although I loved that beautiful city, I still wish to go on living to see other beautiful sights. I won't describe in detail all my experiences, for I have a lot of catching up to do.[13] From Paris we went to London for a few days. Then from Southampton we sailed on the Aquitania *to Halifax. In Halifax we took a train to Montreal.*

Only one boy from the whole group appealed to me. He [Steve Nasser] was very handsome, with dark hair and eyes and even features. At first he didn't seem to take notice of me. Then one day we happened to be seated next to each other on the train. We started talking and really hit it off.

Some details of a book I recently read came to my mind. One woman asks another, who is adored by many men, how to make a conquest: Let him speak about himself, his childhood, about the clever tricks he played at school, and so on; don't interrupt, possibly say a few praising,

---

12 Susan wrote this section of her diary in Hungarian and translated it into English later in her life.

13 Susan had arrived in Canada on August 23, 1948.

encouraging words. After one such conversation, the deed is done. Well, if this was the trick, it worked, though I didn't realize it at the time. When we arrived in Montreal, he helped me off with my luggage. Another girl [Mari] and I were getting off there, while the rest of the group was going on to Toronto. Mari had a friend in Montreal and I was going on to Vegreville.

I was almost overwhelmed with despair. A horrible ice-cold fear took hold of me. Now there were the two of us. Soon I would be utterly alone. I didn't want to cry; I gritted my teeth in order to hold back my tears. Steve gave me a four-leaf clover for good luck, to remember him by. Then they left. Perhaps we will meet again sometime in the future. By then, probably, it won't matter.

We spent two horrible days in Montreal. It took no more than that for the few Hungarians we met there to enlighten us about our bleak prospects. Everyone rues the day they left home. They don't earn enough and everyone takes advantage of the foreigners. I still had hope. I was going to a family. Mari, the other girl, said she would take the next boat home if she could. As for me, even my hopes were filled with fear.

The hour arrived for me to leave. Mari could not accompany me to the airport because the taxi would be too expensive. Thus, we said goodbye and I remained alone with a less-than-sympathetic lady with whom I could converse only in English. As I could do no more than babble in that tongue, I was doubly unhappy. She gave me some cheap candy, which I gave to the cleaning lady just the other day.

When the plane first took off I didn't feel a thing; I just heard an ear-splitting rumbling sound. Later we were served lunch. That was one meal in my life I regretted consuming. As we were approaching Winnipeg, the plane began to descend while my stomach started to heave. I took powerful breaths, promising myself that under no circumstances would I vomit — a promise I could not have kept a minute longer had we not arrived just then on the ground. In Winnipeg I had to transfer planes. There I was met by someone who told me that the person meeting me in Edmonton could speak Hungarian.

I fell asleep on the plane at around 10:00 [a.m.]. At 12:00 I was awakened by the stewardess, who informed me that we were about to arrive. Hovering between sleep and wakefulness, the thought crossed my mind that nothing really matters. I can sleep anywhere. This thought soothed me.

A lady of about forty and a young man of about twenty were waiting for me. My first question addressed to the lady was whether she could speak Hungarian. It was very embarrassing, as it turned out that this was the lady I was going to live with. No, she could not speak Hungarian.

We came here [to Vegreville] *by car. They* [the Kleins] *have a very nice house. I have a room of my own. On the dresser there are pictures of their two sons. One* [Allan] *is in Winnipeg going to medical school; the other* [Hymie] *is in the Haganah. I looked at the pictures, took a bath and fell asleep without a thought. I didn't even count the corners of the room in my new home.*

The next day, Mr. Klein showed me around. I wanted to like the place. It is a very inviting, clean little place. It has one main street, where all the stores are located. But the rest has a villagey character. Mostly family homes with gardens. He also showed me their store.

The first day that I had to shave under my armpits, I was fitted with a bra. I must have scraped myself, because I was very uncomfortable.

Mr. and Mrs. Klein were really nice to me. Altogether there are only six Jewish families here. Not even one girl, which is really too bad.

In the first few weeks, I constantly tried to tell myself that everything was dandy and I was very happy. Then school started. I found it very discouraging.

Then the thought occurred to me that I am not tied to here and I don't have to talk myself into something I don't believe in. From that moment on, I did not have one peaceful moment. I could not see myself staying here but I had no idea how I would convey this to them [the Kleins]. *I could not sleep a wink and I had constant headaches. I was terribly despairing. Finally I decided to tell them. But how? Only God could help me here. I could barely speak a few words of English; how could I explain how I feel? Finally I did. I was still faced with another hard problem. "Why do you want to leave?" Dear me, how could I answer this, when I did not know myself? I just knew that things were not right for me here. At home I was completely independent; I could come and go as I pleased. I went to the theatre, opera, movies. I had girlfriends who visited me and I could visit them. Here there is no theatre, no opera and no friends. They persistently and determinedly tried to talk me out of it. I, just the same, was sticking to my guns. Strange as it may sound, I feel they are speaking in their own interests, not only in mine. How embarrassing for them if I leave! Maybe I just suffer from an overactive imagination but I believe there is some truth in that. I received a letter from Steve that I could go to school in Toronto. I needn't worry about that* [going to school].

I had to write a letter to the head of the [Canadian Jewish] *Congress to ask him to make arrangements on my behalf. In order to do this, I went through real hell. I finally succeeded in having the letter written and sent to the proper place. From then on I grew calm and felt better. Now I believed it was just a question of time. It's impossible for them to deny my request knowing how I feel. In a week I received the reply. They will not pay for me to go to Toronto. However, if after all that happened the Kleins don't want to keep me, I could possibly go to Edmonton. I felt cast down. I could not imagine what would happen next. What happened was that Mr. Klein suggested I stay there to finish the year, after which he would arrange for me to go to Toronto and go to school. I was silent.*

The following day, the Kleins were going to Edmonton, and they said they would talk to the representative of the Congress who was there at the time. When they returned, they told me not to be frightened if I found a strange man in the house. On the way home from school I wondered who they could have brought home with them from Edmonton. The thought shot through me suddenly that it must be the representative from the Congress. I entered the house resolved to deal with anything. I just wanted this unlucky afternoon to be concluded. A man

stood up from the sofa and asked, "Are you Susan? I am Mr. Jabrukow."
He questioned me, but very considerately. He let me talk. I told him I
could not bear to stay here. My life is agony ever since I've been here.

When the Kleins returned from the store, they were having a seri-
ous discussion that I was sure concerned me. They must send me to
Toronto. There cannot be anything else.

What got into me I am unable to say. I decided that I will stay.
Rather than lose the school year, I will endure my year here. In the
meantime I was getting letters from Steve and I gathered from his words
how much he wished that I were in Toronto. I let him know that I would
stay for the school year. He replied that he would remain without a
companion if he could be sure he is not waiting in vain.

October 26

On Yom Kippur night I went to a hall. I had a fairly good time, con-
sidering. Everyone said I looked very pretty. By the way, Eli took me
dancing twice. And his brother took me to the Expo and we ran into
him there. I didn't win anything. He said that means I am lucky in love.
Yesterday I was loathsome to him. All the Jewish families were together
to have dinner. Everyone was drinking except me because I don't like
alcohol. I told him I didn't like people who drink. He asked me if I liked
him and I said "no" with a straight face. By the way, there is a nut here
who keeps telling me that were he fifteen years younger, I would not
have a free moment. I retorted that I was glad he wasn't.

When Eli took me home, he promised never to drink again. I have
no idea why! I never asked him to. Then he said that he is not lucky in
love because he won in the games of luck.

October 28

The day before yesterday we went to Edmonton, to attend a party. I
had a terrible time. Mostly older people were there but they acted too
young. I met the Kleins' daughter-in-law [Queena] there. She is very
charming.

The next day I went to Irene's. I went to the Yom Kippur ball[14] with her cousin. I felt bad because I thought he took me because he had to, because I don't know anyone in Edmonton. But later on at the dance, somehow I thought that he did like me. At the last dance, he came over and asked my partner to let him have this dance with me. Though this is not the custom here, he said he wanted to have the last dance with me. When we came home, he asked me to come to Edmonton for the next dance.

Irene told me that when the kids were discussing who should go with whom, he [her cousin] immediately said he would take me. Then when someone else said he would, he said that if he is not taking me, he is staying at home.

I don't know what is the matter with me, but I don't think I can stand such a life much longer. There is no joy in it. My greatest happiness is to receive a letter. When I don't, it's a hundred times worse. Everything is a pain from morning to night, without a let-up. How I hate this town and everybody! I don't especially like the Kleins. Mrs. Klein is not very friendly sometimes. Mr. Klein is really nice, but somehow he is not a real gentleman.

If only it weren't for that cursed money problem, how much happier I would be! Sometimes I think I will make my wishes dependent upon their son coming home from Palestine. I heard such nice things about him, I like him already. I do get crazy ideas.

That is not to say, whatever will be will be, but as of yet I have not decided what I really want and I will not torture myself as I was doing in the beginning. I am sure some decision will be formed in my own mind, and I will know what my goal is.

---

14 An anti-religious or alternative activity originally created by Jewish anarchists in the late 1800s in England and New York.

November 1

It's frustrating that I cannot put down in writing things the way I really feel them. Maybe because by the time I sit down to write, the feeling is gone. I was glad about something and I wanted to describe it in detail, but I don't anymore.

I dreamt that I loved someone and was loved in return. I've never yet had such a happy and peaceful feeling.

I was awakened at 8:45 and got a lift to school; I wasn't even late. Cruel awakening. All day I was daydreaming. Now I have no feeling left.

It's strange and exasperating that I have no friends and no hope for any. I don't even have the assurance that things will be all right if I go to Toronto. How can I count on Steve feeling the same way as in the beginning? We barely know each other, really. Our short friendship isn't nearly enough to nourish it for a year. But something will surely turn up. Quoting my favourite saying, "Valahogy csak lesz, mert úgy még sohasem volt, hogy sehogy sem lett volna."[15]

November 11

I received a letter from Helga saying she wants to come to Canada.[16] I can't describe how happy I would be if, indeed, she comes. The Kleins write her that she could get a job in Edmonton. What's more, they said that if any members of my family want to come to Canada, they will guarantee for them. Poor things, they don't know what they offer to undertake. Many members of my family have an adventurous spirit. [My cousin] *Bandi's* [family] *wants to go to Palestine. I wrote them to come here. Oh, if whatever I wish would come true!*

---

15 "Somehow it will, because it has never been so that it never was." Mihály Babits.
16 Helga is the daughter of Susan's grandmother's brother. She managed to leave Hungary during the war by going to England to work as a maid.

Today Bernie asked me to go dancing. I told him no. I hope he won't pester me again. He does not appeal to me in the least.

On Sunday all the Edmontonians are coming here for a party. I wonder what it will be like.

November 15

The party took place yesterday. It wasn't bad, but it was too crowded. The young people went to the Hardins' to play ping-pong. Then one of the boys played the piano and we danced. I wasn't really enjoying myself.

It's strange, but although I may be smiling during the day, at night I truly feel my heart. Perhaps it's not even Steve, himself, but he is the only, only human being in Canada I would like to be with.

Yesterday I did something that was probably very stupid. The Kleins said, why doesn't Steve come here? He could work or go to school here if he wants. So I wrote and asked him. I don't believe he'll come. He will feel the same as I do. In one way, he may want to come, but he would have to throw away something he has for certain. Now, he is in a good place. In spite of seeing all this clearly, if he said no, it would be awful for me. I would lose the one thing I am holding onto. I have more to lose than him — though that's not the important thing. If he writes that he won't come, or can't come, then I won't [go] either, as much as I would want to, and I will remain alone. Now I can still indulge in daydreams. How it would be and what it would be like if we were together. Anywhere. But if not, I am left only with nightmares.

Sometimes, while I read or write — possibly it has to do with on what subject — I am suddenly transported back home, doing the same thing long ago. It appears so real for a second that I am no longer here. In the next moment, my heart sinks and it's over.

November 21

I received Steve's reply. When I heard I had a letter from Toronto, I ran to the store, right to the office, and while holding the letter in my hand,

I thought, "Don't dream that he'll come. This would make you happier than you have the right to be." I tore the letter open. I scanned through it quickly and the only thing I understood was "I am coming." How can I explain how I feel? I felt as though I was in heaven. How will I be able to sit through school this afternoon? Then the more practical questions arose in my mind. How will he come? Will he acquire wings to fly here? Mrs. Klein says that if he wants to come he can pay for it. Even if he has the money, he needs it to establish a new life. We'll see what will happen.

November 23
Helga wrote that she may be arriving around the end of December.

November 24
How I hate to be here! How I hate everybody! Did I give up my life at home to come here? I wanted change, adventure, and I am here in this awfulness. I want so much to do something, to be somebody, to travel, to see different things, to live a colourful life. But I must stay here. Should I spend my whole life here? Should I have Steve come here for my sake? Maybe Helga can advise me when she comes.

I cannot imagine living such a vacant, barren life as most people seem to: live, work, struggle, marry. Some may succeed in acquiring certain things, yet are grinding up their youth doing it. I don't want such a life. I don't.

January 15, 1949
During Christmas I spent three days in Calgary. Coincidentally, I met a girl there who also went to the Jewish gimnázium *[in Budapest]. I told her all my problems and it was a release at the time. Later on I was mad at myself, but all in all I felt better after I let off some steam.*

I went to a New Year's party in Edmonton. I had a terrible time. But I am the only one to blame. I simply cannot communicate with the kids here. A boy who asked who I was when I was here once before took me. At first I liked him, maybe I still do. It was awful. The girls were sitting in the boys' laps and in honour of the New Year everybody kissed everybody. Maybe I am too romantic but I always imagined that when I kiss for the first time I will be in love and will be very happy. Everybody must have thought I was crazy, and I was very uncomfortable. We and another couple went to another room and were kissing, without feeling or meaning. I think everyone felt the same way, just wanted to act more like adults than they really are. I had to do it, I simply had to. For a week after, I was chewing myself out I was so ashamed. I began to think I am very stupid. Why do I feel so lost in the company of young people? How will this end?

I got a letter from Helga today. She is now leaving at the end of February. I have my hope in her in all respects. The Kleins are talking about me going to Edmonton next year and going to business college and taking ballet lessons. I am double-jointed, so I am very flexible — one talent I may achieve something with.

My God, how I wish to break out from the confines of a human existence. But it's not possible that I won't go to high school. I am capable and want to fulfill that potential, too. Even if I have to study all night, I will go to high school. I don't want to be like I was at the New Year's party, awkward and stupid. I want to be proud and assured and I want a good life. I want it so much that I will succeed.

July 22
Hymie came home a few days before Passover. He is a very nice and warm person. I really like him. It's silly, but I need to like somebody. In all likelihood everyone here thinks I am very cold. Somehow nothing makes me happy and I love no one. I think that the latter is the reason for the former, and the reason for the latter is being conscious of the fact that no one really cares for me. Perhaps some could take advantage of this situation — no need to consider anyone. But I can't live like this for long.

Helga arrived just in time for the first seder. We were invited to the Versoffs and we brought her along with us. They brought gifts for all the children and as she was reported to be my cousin they believed she was a young girl and got her a gift, too.

She stayed in Vegreville for a week. This was my Easter vacation and of course my great plans for studying all went up in smoke. But it was worth it — though I am still hoping for the best regarding the result of my exams. I had a chance to talk to someone, though we quarrelled and argued a lot. But at least I had a chance to get [my anger] out of my system for the whole year.

After Helga went to Edmonton and started working, I still didn't study. Olyan's granddaughter, Lynn Shapiro, came for a visit from Calgary. We spent a lot of time together. Wherever we went, that stupid Bernie seemed to be following us around. He phoned the other day to ask if I was going to camp. I said I didn't think so. Then he asked whether it would make any difference if he were going. Then I said I wasn't going.

In the meantime, Lynn developed a crush on Hymie and kept talking about him all the time, until I got tired of liking him — which is a good thing. But I still consider him the nicest, kindest adoptive brother.

The next few weeks were spent studying because the dreaded exams were approaching. The graduation ball was on June 3. It seems silly to me to celebrate graduation before graduating. I would rather have stayed home and read or slept. I went because of everyone's insistence. Bernie invited me two months before the ball. I said it was still far away and there was a lot of time to think about it. A month later I still gave him a non-committal answer. At home I announced that I wasn't going. Mrs. Klein said I could do no such thing. Everyone will be there, and they want to go, too. The best thing about the ball was the beautiful light blue taffeta dress I got to wear.

On the second of June, a really cute thing happened to me. Around 7:00 p.m. I finally decided to sit down to study. To my chagrin, Mrs.

Klein asked me to put on my yellow dress because she wanted to see it on me. Inwardly I was having temper tantrums — firstly, because I wanted to study, secondly, because it didn't make any sense. But no, I must do as told. Little Susan put on the dress. The next request was to put on a white slip. Now I became stubborn and refused. In the end I put on a half-slip. Next I had to put on white shoes. By now I was seeing stars. Then she asked me to take a plate of pastry over to the neighbours. I said, all right, but first I will change back into my comfortable jeans. She was strongly protesting against this, saying that Mrs. Irvine wants to make a similar dress for Lorraine and wants to see it. So I took the pastry and was about to turn around and go home, assuming that the dress wasn't really important, when Lorraine asked me to come in for a few minutes. All my studies and the dream of my exams were flashing through my mind and I was about to refuse, but I thought better of it — it would not be very polite. The first thing I noticed was that the carpets were not on the floor and a few little girls were sitting on the sofa in solemn silence; only Lorraine's gramophone, which she got for her birthday, was playing heartily. "Are you having a party?" I asked her. "No, you are having one. It's a surprise party for you," she replied. This thoughtfulness really touched me while I was dancing with thirteen-year-old little boys.

While I was opening the gifts, I felt very embarrassed, which I hope passed for happiness. The Kleins deserved that at least I should appear so. They gave me a bike and I got many other gifts from the Irvines and the other kids. From the Hardins and Tunises I got a really sweet box of writing paper.

This was my first birthday [party], which, in spite of all appearances, I spent alone. I wonder where I will spend the next one.

I wasn't nervous at all while I was writing my exams. I could hardly believe how calm I was. But that didn't prevent me from spoiling my English literature exam. I knew I didn't have enough time. I started everything, re-did everything, and didn't complete anything. I hope the grammar part will bring up my average. If I pass, I have to give Mr. Finlay credit for it. He had a high opinion of me and his confidence in me kept up my spirits.

After I finished writing my exams I went to Calgary to visit Ibi Bein. On Tuesday I found out that on Thursday I could get a ride there. I quickly wrote her a short note and mailed it, but I wasn't sure she would receive it in time. We arrived at her house at about 1:00 a.m. I had visions of a sleepy-looking man in pyjamas coming to the door and angrily telling me to go away, and slamming the door in my face. As luck or unluck would have it, they were up and they were having some visitors stay with them. For this reason, there were no extra beds, and I had to sleep in a single bed with Ibi, whose expanse is fairly extensive. I myself am about five pounds overweight, which I finally decided to shed.

On the first day we went on a picnic with a few other refugee girls. We had a very nice time, but at the moment it's not girls I am interested in. I met a boy here at Christmas time who reminds me of Steve. He could barely speak a few words of English then but said that by the time we meet again, he would [be speaking more English]. *He called me and we went dancing. We also made plans for the next day, on account of which Ibi and I had a gigantic argument. We are either arguing, laughing, singing or reciting poems together.*

Thinking about laughing reminds me of a cute incident. Earl Hardin took me dancing once. He is a smart boy but acts like a blockhead sometimes. At the door, he asked, "Susie, will you kiss me goodnight?" This came so unexpectedly that I surprised myself by giving him a peck and ran in. Inside, the situation hit me as so funny that I was rolling on the floor laughing. The Kleins thought I was out of my mind.

The Smiths, the people Ibi is staying with, were going to Banff. They were begging us to go with them. But I was expecting a phone call and didn't want to go. Ibi would have liked to go but couldn't because of my obstinance. When Robi phoned, the problem of finding a date for Ibi arose. But finally we solved the Gordian knot without the help of Alexander the Great[17] and we went to the park for a boat ride. Robi

17 A metaphor used to describe a complex or entangled issue, associated with a legend dating back to 333 BCE and Alexander the Great.

asked for my address in case he can visit me one day, but I forgot to give it to him. He asked me again at the party, but again I forgot.

Another boy took me out a few times, but he started to bore me and when he phoned again, I said I was busy.

Ibi and I often stay up till three, four o'clock in the morning, gabbing and reciting poems to each other.

I saw Lynn, who wanted me to stay with her for a week. But I don't want to because I must start working and earning some money. Though at night I always have something to do, the days are pretty long. My biggest thrill here was finding the record Yiddishe Mame. *I bought it, and I sent it to Mrs. Klein for her birthday with another record. I had looked for this record all over Edmonton for Mother's Day, to no avail. When I found it here, I was in veritable ecstasy.*

Hymie was also vacationing here. The first time he came to visit, he took us to a Jewish camp near by. It is located by a lake, with motorboats and sailboats. It must be fantastic to be there for a while. He also took me to the [Stampede] parade. It was sweltering hot and two huge men stood in front of me, under whose armpits I was trying to see. Finally they took pity on me and let me stand in front of them. I found the Indians most interesting. It was the first time I saw authentic Indians.[18]

Lynn persuaded me to sleep at her house, saying that we would probably not see each other again and we should be together when we could. The next morning I was still in pyjamas when the phone rang and the person who was giving me a ride home [to Edmonton, to stay with Helga] *said that he was leaving in an hour. I promised to be ready. I had to rush like crazy, back to the Smiths, pack and so on. I said goodbye to the Smiths, who were very sweet to me and whom I learned to love. They are very nice and charming people. They gave me a bottle of Chanel* [perfume]. *Their son was so sweet; he presented me with a Stampede flag and promised to write.*

---

18 This was a common way to refer to an Indigenous person; the term is now outdated but kept here for historical accuracy.

July 25

The next morning Helga and I went all over the city looking for a job. The employment agency had openings only for housekeepers. After a while Helga suggested that I might consider that possibility. It sounded pretty bad. I, Susanna Veronica Löffler, a maid. Crazy. On the other hand, as Helga reasoned, it's forty dollars, room and board. I tried to reason it out. I want to work in order to have money. It doesn't matter how I earn it as long as I don't steal it. Helga and I plan to go to Toronto. My plan now is to go take a certain course at the business college, which will guarantee me a good job, and to take high school courses at night. I want to go to Toronto really soon, and for this I need money. Thus, what choice do I have? One choice among one. Easier to say than do. We shall see if I have the stamina and courage of my conviction.

Helga's boss said that he has a personal friend who could probably use me. They have a son and daughter, and they want a babysitter and help with the housework. Having no chance for another kind of job, my pride filed down somewhat, I decided to go to that family to see if I am suitable for them. They thought I looked very young, twelve rather than sixteen. They would give me a week's try, then decide what to pay me, around twenty-five dollars. They seemed very pleasant. Mr. Pulton is the manager of Woolworth's [a discount store].

The next morning Mr. Pulton picked me up. Thus, five days ago I embarked on my life's most beautiful career. Since then, I have been working like a machine. Today Mrs. Pulton asked if I wanted to stay. I said I would (but I would like to know what they decided to pay me). She also offered for me to stay here, go to school and help out with the dishes and babysit. It's really not a bad idea, but I don't want to be a slave. While I am cleaning, the only idea that holds my body and soul together is that the time may not be so far when I will be on a train leaving for Toronto, and the whistle of the train will be sweet music accompanying the singing of my heart. I want this so much I must succeed.

July 27

Often I get so depressed. I am so alone and I have no chance to meet anyone. Today, for instance, I saw some girls I met at the New Year's party. I very cautiously avoided them because I didn't want them to ask me what I am doing. It would be a lie to say I am ashamed only for the Kleins' sake. It's silly, but I can't help it.

Today I decided to ask how much they are going to pay me. Thirty-five dollars and a promise of a raise later. Hurrah! This is more than I would be able to save doing another job.

Tomorrow I am going for a haircut. Helga took on a night job. That means that by October 25 she will be a rich person, the proprietor of three hundred dollars with which to set out for Toronto. It's a beginning.

July 28

I have almost nothing left of my hair. It is very straight and very short — I felt bald. At first I was so upset I was almost in tears. But later, I put some waves into it. It's not so bad. It will grow.

I went to a movie with Helga. It was good, but it had a sad ending; it made me sad, too.

We were having a discussion about the meaning of being Jewish for us. Helga said she would deny it only if it would mean a drawback for her. I don't believe I would do that. I had my share of suffering on account of it. I feel proud to be Jewish and I don't consider myself less than anyone because of it. Indeed, if anything, just the opposite. I once tried to gain advantage by denying it, in vain. I won't try it again. During the Nazi era, Mother and I converted. When she first asked my opinion about it, I expressed strong disapproval. "Perhaps it will save us," she said. That feeble "perhaps" was stronger than anything at the time. I am not ashamed of it, and I don't even consider it having any meaning. We used to go down to the basement, where the priest taught us the catechism. I still remember the Lord's Prayer. I guess that can't hurt.

Lately I think about Steve a lot. It seems to me that for him it's not all that important to have a girlfriend all the time, but that he has deeper feelings [for me]. *I hope my intuition will not deceive me.*

I am writing a book. I already have the rough sketch all laid out. I wonder when I will write the concluding words.

July 30
Last night I went to visit Helga. When I returned, only old Mrs. Pulton was awake. She showed me her pictures and we were talking for a long time. She is a very sweet lady, eighty years old, but she cannot sit still. She is bustling around all the time. Her second husband, who was an old friend, died a year ago. Now she doesn't know what is awaiting her from one day to the next. It seems absurd that I, a sixteen year old, should understand her. I fear old age, to be alone and have no one. This is why I am so scared that the years are flying by without experiencing any happiness.

Helga phoned to let me know that the Kleins returned from their holiday. I wonder if they will want to take me home. I want to tell them my plans. I am very nervous about their reaction to it.

August 2
The clash has occurred. It was more horrible and painful than I could have imagined. I asked Mrs. Pulton to give me the day off because the Kleins were coming to Edmonton for a visit. She let me go, saying I could make up for the time next week.

Helga cooked my favourite dishes. In the afternoon we were suntanning. The two Sauls were there. We were fooling around and one of them jokingly asked me to marry him. In the end he became insolent and kissed me while I was suntanning, for which I slapped him.

The Kleins finally arrived at around 8:00 p.m. With them were Queena and Allan, who were my guardian angels, and I hope they will remain so while I am here.

I told them of my plan to take a computer course, to which Mrs. Klein responded that they had done all they were going to do for me and would not help me any further. I could see troubles ahead, as she was obviously in a very hostile and quarrelsome mood. Why should they help me if I want to go to Toronto? As the atmosphere became more disagreeable, Queena asked me to show her where the washroom was. When we went upstairs she asked me what I really wanted to do. She was very nice and understanding and said she would write to the Congress and see what could be done.

When we went down again, Mrs. Klein was screaming terribly at Helga, "Let her go to the Congress! They will give her nothing, the same as they gave her till now! She is over sixteen now and let her go to work like everyone else!" She was shouting and yelling so much and she was so unnerved that there was no point in arguing with her. Then Allan called me aside and said that though he is almost like a stranger, I should still try to talk to him and tell him what I want. At that point I could not control myself anymore and started crying. He was very nice and seemed to understand me.

As far as my job was concerned, Mr. Klein declared that I could not stay there. To which Mrs. Klein said sarcastically that if I like it, I should stay. Mr. Klein was very nice, still trying to talk me out of going to Toronto, questioning what I would be doing there. But in any case he said I should quit my job and go home with them, to which Mrs. Klein gave him some murderous glances. Mrs. Klein said they will buy me a ticket to Toronto and to expect nothing more from them. Then they left. I will endure it all, but I must do what I want.

Helga walked me to the bus stop and we were discussing things over and over again. All of a sudden she asked me what I believe about the afterlife. I answered jokingly, but meant seriously, that I believe the worms will eat me. I don't believe in an afterlife. This is why I think it's so important to have a full life in this world and not to waste it. To this she replied that I will succeed because I don't care how much pain I cause along the way. I just strive toward my own dream. I broke my grandmother's heart and Malvin's heart when I came to Canada. Now I am causing the Kleins pain. But she thinks I am smart doing what I want, and she respects me for it. I retorted that I learned from bitter experience that one should do what is best for oneself. My father didn't want to leave his mother. He was a good son. But is he a good son and a good father now?

Mr. Klein phoned me and told me that I had failed my exams. Somehow I knew he was just teasing me; it would have been too terrible to be true. "You got an A average," he said. I couldn't even believe it and I won't until I see it for myself. I had to tell someone quickly, so I phoned Helga and I wrote home.

August 6

The Kleins phoned yesterday and said that I should take the bus home, as they will probably not come in on Sunday. When I arrived, I went to the store first thing to get my mail. I saw my report card and I really believe my marks. I also got several postcards from Malvin and Auntie Magda. They are on vacation and are having a good time. I also got a picture of Kathy and Susie. Bandi named her after me; that is, they wanted to have a Susie in the family. She actually looks a little bit like me. It's so strange, I was so close to them, and now I can't even see those babies.

Again I was preached to, and I listened without any reaction. I just keep saying they are right. They must think I am crazy. When I first arrived Mrs. Klein was a little cold. We didn't know how to behave with each other after all the hysterics the time before.

August 11

Yesterday I got up at about 9:30. We were supposed to be going to Edmonton by 10:00. At around 11:30 Mr. Klein came home, called Mrs. Klein aside and they were whispering. This appeared to me very suspicious because he never comes home at this time. They must be talking about me. In all probability they have an answer from the Congress and it's not good news. Otherwise they would tell me. I felt a helpless rage against them because I felt they were not fair to me. They probably wrote [Congress] *that they meant to send me to school and they did everything for me, but that I don't want to stay. As recently as two weeks ago and as far back as Christmas all I hear about is business college, not high school. In any case, my English is not nearly good enough for shorthand* [taking dictation].

As soon as I returned from Calgary at Christmas time, they received me with the news that they talked to Mr. Finlay, who said that one can go to business college after completing Grade 9. I was very upset then. Just last week Mrs. Klein said, "If you pass or not, we have a plan for you. You'll go to college and then to work." But I don't want to go to college. I want to go to high school. But to return to the subject at hand, I had the feeling that the reply arrived from the Congress, which is unfavourable, and I was blaming them. What strengthened my belief was that when Hymie phoned and asked for Mr. Klein and I went to look for him, they were reading a letter. Then Allan came home and they were having a discussion in Yiddish. Later on he came over to me and said, "Do you know you are a famous girl?" I did not know. In fact I really got scared because I didn't know what he meant. But I had no reason to be scared. There was an article about me in the newspaper regarding my exams.[19]

In Edmonton I dropped in to see Helga, but only for a few minutes because she was busy at work. Then I went to the Bergers and suntanned there. When Helga came home I told her about my dream the night before. A wild animal was chasing me. Often I dream such things. I am in a field with many other people and suddenly everyone is running and wolves are chasing us. I hide, but I know I will be found and I am very scared. Helga says she will have it analyzed. I am curious what it means.

I also told her about my suspicions about the letter. I told her I will have to ask if they received an answer from the Congress and will let her know as soon as possible.

---

19 A clip from the article can be found on page 181.

I saw a wonderful movie called Enchantment. *It was a romantic love story. It just suited my mood and taste. When I went back to the Bergers, the Kleins were already waiting for me. We had tea and left for home. In the car I asked them if they got an answer from the Congress. They said they did. They will get in touch with Toronto to find out if they have a place for me. If not, they will send me to Winnipeg. It would be horrid if after all the arguing and fighting I would end up in Winnipeg. Why would I go to Winnipeg?*

August 12

Yesterday I went horseback riding. It was divine! It was in a magnificent, romantic setting, in the thick of the forest, so that I had to bend away the branches of the trees to not get scratched. I had a little old horse who was moving slowly, but I let it, in order to enjoy the beauty of the landscape, and he did not throw me off his back. But later on, he frightened me. He became disobedient and as we were returning, at any price he wanted to return with me to the stable. I was protesting because I still wanted to go on, but then I understood that the poor thing must have been hungry, so I let him go on his way.

This afternoon I was suntanning. I am also on a diet. I only have two weeks left and I want to look nice when I arrive in Toronto. I am still hoping for the best.

August 13

Yesterday we were freezing peas. I had been shelling them while I was suntanning. With great determination, I did not touch my supper. "Tell me, how can you sit at the table and watch people eat?" [Mrs. Klein said.] "You do have willpower."

Later on I opened my box that contains my memorabilia from home — old letters, poems, some of which I wrote, others that were written by more famous individuals. This was the first time I opened the envelope containing the four-leaf clover Steve gave me when they went to Toronto and I remained in Montreal, the postcard from the boat with all the kids' signatures with whom I came, the diary that I started when I was eleven and which contains more or less everything that has happened to me until I came to Canada.

In the evening we went to a movie called Key Largo starring Humphrey Bogart. It was very good but so heavy that it literally sat on me. But it was a very good story and the characterization was a true masterpiece of art.

After we came home, we started a discussion about the value of the dollar. "Why is it that though Canada is so rich in wealth, the American dollar is more valuable?" I asked.

"Because the population is small," replied Mr. Klein.

"Then why don't they allow larger immigration? Perhaps it would have been better if the government did change in the last election."

"The fault isn't in the government but in the world's system. Capitalism has had its day; the people are not grand enough, not idealistic enough to get rid of the system and bring in true socialism," said Mr. Klein.

"But we have democracy here in Canada. All I hear about is Canadian democracy."

"Nonsense," said Mrs. Klein. "Where is democracy? A few rich and powerful people are in charge of the world and they invent trouble and war in order to avert attention from themselves. And the people are materialistic rather than idealistic."

We've had a few such discussions and I cannot figure out what they really believe in. It seems to me that they change their minds.

The next day I wanted to suntan but it was cloudy and changeable weather. The sun peeked out from behind the clouds only occasionally and from time to time trivial short storms started and stopped.

When Hymie came home I told him that I thought the weather is so changeable and crazy.

[He said,] "Supposedly it has a good influence on people's brains and their ability to work."

"How is Canada an example in this regard?" I questioned. There is practically not a poet, writer or artist of importance born in Canada.

"Don't forget Canada is a new country. It does not have a two-thousand-year history like the European countries."

I accepted this reasoning, though how does a country's history affect a human being's talent?

August 14

I often muse and am a little discouraged, being conscious of the fact that I see so few happy people. And people, couples, seem to make each other's lives so bitter, without a reason, so stupidly. Through just a little understanding they could accomplish such a great deal to be happy. And every human being, without exception, prays for this, but they are unwilling to make the smallest sacrifice to secure it. It is so discouraging, people's foolishness and callousness against the very people they are close to and they love. Where is understanding, tact, good will, nice words?

Today, being Sunday, is cleaning day. I got up early to be finished early. The weather being bad, I was sewing and listening to the radio. My things are pretty neglected and I want to get everything in good order before I leave.

At 6:00 I went for a swim. After that I went to the Tunises to get the things I left there while I was staying with them. They were trying to convince me of my foolishness in wanting to leave, but after a while they gave up on me.

Then I was reading. I find this book particularly interesting. It is the story of a Jewish boy who goes to America from Russia. I find it all the more interesting as I can identify with it in many respects.

August 15

The result of my reading until all hours was that I got up late. I washed my hair and waved it with my fingers. Mrs. Klein was so pleased because since I've been here she's been trying to convince me to do this instead of curling my hair.

In the afternoon I read. I didn't eat any supper again.

"Why are you doing this? What are you trying to accomplish with this starvation?" asked Mr. Klein.

"She wants to be slim, dark and have curly white-blond hair," answered Mrs. Klein.

After supper I did the dishes, sewed, ironed, read. Now I am writing, and now that I am finished, I will read again.

I finally sent birthday cards to Éva and Ági and I bought a potato peeler for Mrs. Klein. I, too, can use it while I am still here.

August 23

Last Wednesday I went to Edmonton. I got a letter from Steve. He wrote that someone from the Congress phoned him regarding me and mainly, whatever gave them the idea to call him? I have no idea why and how. I wonder what the Kleins wrote to the Congress.

Helga asked me to stay with her for a few days over the weekend, to be together for the last time till God knows when. I gladly agreed, on the condition that she doesn't bug me about my diet, because I want to lose weight. So all that week I was on an apple and cornflake diet. I was suntanning and from 6:00 to 7:00 in the evening I visited Helga.

It was arranged that at 1:00 p.m. on Saturday I meet her at the office, we look around in the stores for a short while, then go to a movie. First, I took my bike to the C P R [Canadian Pacific Railway]. I had left it at the office on the previous day, so that I wouldn't have to drag it with me. All of a sudden, Helga ran into one of her colleagues. Then the two of them started running around looking at things and I was following after them. After a while I was getting pretty tired and angry. They tried on a bunch of dresses and Helga bought one, which looked very good on her. Then we went for lunch. At first I thought that although I had eaten my diet lunch, consisting of an apple, I might eat a sandwich for a change. When we arrived at the restaurant, Helga told me to sit down on a bench by the wall. I didn't mind; truthfully, I was glad that now I didn't have to break my diet, but at the same time I was slightly annoyed. Then Helga returned and said that now there was room by the table. I said I didn't want to eat. Then her friend came over and tried to talk me into eating. Now on top of my anger I was getting nervous too because I had to stay polite amidst this useless arguing, as I knew I wasn't going to eat. Again Helga came and said to sit with them and eat. I repeated that I wouldn't eat. She said, no matter, I should sit with them anyway, which I then did. All of a sudden the waitress comes and brings me a big order of ice-cream sundae. I told Helga I wasn't eating it. Then let it stay, she said. Okay, I agreed. But that cost a lot of money, she said. But I told you I wasn't eating, I said. Go home, I don't want you here, she said. Goodbye, I answered, and left and went home. Later she phoned to ask if I wanted to go to the movie. I didn't answer.

What am I, a little dog that she can dismiss and recall at her will? But I did so want to go the movie. I had been alone all week and was looking forward to it... now I can again sit at home all afternoon. To top it off I remembered that Malvin wrote that she had written to Fred's sister in Paris to try to take some steps on my behalf [to get to Toronto]. *I thought that this might only cause more problems for me. I was so depressed and despairing that I would have liked to smash or break something.*

At 8:00 p.m. I phoned Irene to ask her if she would like to go to the movies. I borrowed a dollar from Fanny and went. We had to wait in line for an hour to get in [to see *Little Women*] *but it was worth it. I got home at 1:00 in the morning. Helga was already sleeping. The next morning she was very unfriendly and I decided that if she wants to act like such a baby, let her. But in the end we started talking and explained the reasons for our conduct. What's more, she went as far as to say that we could live together, but she doesn't know me well enough. Thus, now we are on most friendly terms.*

On Monday morning, early, I got a lift back to Vegreville. The long, boring days are continuing. Often everything looks pretty dim.

Last night we went to a movie. Tonight we were playing cards. Now Mrs. Klein and I are on very good terms. Hopefully, while I am here, she won't go into more hysterics. Last night I dreamt that I was home and that I saw Ilus, Ági, Fred, Auntie Magda, Uncle Lajos and Susie Löwy. I was in our old apartment and I cried bitterly. I woke in a very depressed mood.

August 25

Yesterday I got up late, and all afternoon I was reading magazines. After supper I decided to go for a walk as, of late, I am always sitting at home. When I returned, I said that I had a lot of washing to do. Mrs. Klein replied that I better do it because they had gotten a telegram from [Congress in] Winnipeg to send me there right away. They haven't yet heard from Toronto.… I said that I know they are taking steps in this regard as Steve wrote me that they phoned him there. I was curious about her reaction to this.

"What do you think will happen?" I asked. "Perhaps we'll know more on Sunday," she answered. They haven't even sent a ticket yet. Also it costs extra to send the luggage. If they don't hear soon they will wire [send a message]. A little while later she asked whether I would want to go to Edmonton. I said yes, I would like to say goodbye to some of the people. "For that reason it's a good idea to go on Sunday, when everyone is at home. But if you want, you can go with Hymie on Friday."

I wanted to tell her that I love them all and how sorry I am to leave them and also that I am very anxious to leave because I want to start school some way, any way or another. But I didn't say anything, possibly because there is such a discrepancy between the two thoughts.

"It would be interesting if you left this Sunday. It would be exactly a year to the day you arrived."

Today I asked whether they received a letter yet from Winnipeg. "No," was the answer, and they changed the subject. I cannot understand why they cannot be truthful about this and talk about it. It's been more than a week now since I've been sitting here and every minute of every hour of every day I am waiting for this letter so that I may be able to leave. I don't understand what they want and would like to know what they think.

Last night I dreamt that I arrived in Toronto and Steve was waiting for me. He kissed me and I wasn't really sure if I liked him. To tell the truth, I have great fears within myself.

August 26

"I don't want to offend you, but I would like to know, just between the two of us, tell me honestly, why didn't you help out at all, when you first arrived?" asked Mrs. Klein last night.

This question confused and embarrassed me and I didn't know how to answer it. What I remember is that I was doing the dishes on the very first day I was here, and Sundays were spent cleaning up the house. I remember this particularly as this made me feel sad and disappointed as at home I had spent Saturdays and Sundays with my friends. Those were my especially fun days when we went hiking and picnicking or to the swimming pool, or wherever my mood desired.

"I really don't know; I think I don't remember exactly." At home I wasn't required to do anything and probably I didn't realize what I was supposed to do. From this, the conversation turned to my leaving and I told her all the nice things I meant to say. That I love them very much and it hurts me to leave them but I was excessively lonely here and that is why I cannot spend another year here. She answered that from that point of view she understands me, as she would like to leave here too, but everyone asks why I am leaving, what is the exact reason for it, and they don't know what to answer. Finally the truth comes out. I had a feeling that deep down, at the bottom of things, this was part of the problem, vanity on their part. I said, I am going to school no matter what, no matter what sacrifice I have to make to accomplish it.

I was supposed to go to Edmonton today with Hymie and return with them on Sunday. But in the end Hymie wasn't going. I wanted to take the bus, saying I wanted to do certain things that I couldn't on Sunday. I was all ready to go when they declared that I should not go; rather, I should go with them on Sunday and remain until Thursday if I want because it was Herschy Hardin's bar mitzvah the next day. And on Wednesday, when they only work half the day, they will be able to help me pack, and then I can leave.

I was not in the mood to argue. I am not in the mood to go to a bar mitzvah but I see that not going would be very bad manners, uncivil on my part. Thus, tonight we went to a movie, which wasn't very good, and after we played cards.

August 28

On Saturday afternoon I went to the store and stayed there until 6:00 p.m. Then I got ready and we went to the Hardins' to the bar mitzvah party. Several speeches were made and then the young people went upstairs. One of the Hardins' nephews, whom I noticed looking at me, came over and said that he heard that I was going to Edmonton. Where was I staying and would he mind if he called me? I said, not at all. Then another boy came over and said he heard I was going to Toronto and was it true. I said I did not know yet and I had no idea where I would be. He said he would find me. Then they left. Later on I went for a walk with Helen Goldsand, and then with Eli. He asked me again why I didn't want to stay here. In an attack of honesty I decided to tell him what I thought. Also I thought he wanted to kiss me, which I was trying to avoid. I felt that because when I came here I couldn't speak English, I made a bad impression that now I cannot change. Just ask anybody who was at that New Year's party. They must think I am stupid because I wasn't willing to kiss everyone there.

We talked about these things before. He said that he doesn't go out with shikses [non-Jews], but he dated a Jewish girl and they were always necking and they had a good time. I said that to me, to kiss someone who you don't love, just to pass the time, is not appealing.

Later on I said that I had something of his I wanted to return, referring to the ring [he gave to me after I arrived in Vegreville]. Then he said that in a few years' time he will come to Toronto and propose to me, hoping I will not be married already. We spoke about many other things. I felt he respected me for having strong morals. When we

returned everyone was just leaving. Then Earl showed me the Vegreville Observer, *which had the article about me that was written by Mr.
Finlay. It made me feel good to read all the nice things he said about me.*

*Today at noon we started out for Edmonton. On the way there Mr.
and Mrs. Klein had a terrible argument over the very important matter of who should drive the car. I can't even say how horrible I felt. It
is excruciating how petty people are, over what petty things they make
each other miserable.*

*When we arrived we were told that a boy had called for me twice
already. One minute later the phone rang again and this boy asked if I
wanted to go to the baseball game. I said yes. In an hour's time he arrived along with a boy from Toronto in a very ancient, shaky car. It was
actually fun to rattle in it after the new DeSoto. The shaking reminded
me of the No. 6 streetcar at home. We drove around the city and were
chatting a lot. The boy from Toronto made a date with me to meet me
on September 11 at 10:00 in front of the public library. By then we will
probably both forget. I had a good time with them, but thank God I
did not especially like either of them. They wanted to take me to a wedding dance but I said I wasn't dressed properly for it. They suggested
that they invite a few more people and we should go to their place and
dance. I said that if they do get some others, phone me and pick me up.
But then it got too late and they said they would phone me the next day.*

September 1
On Monday after lunch I went shopping for things I needed. I went to
Dowers [Dower Brothers] *where* [my friend] *Helen works and bought
toothpaste, face cream and other odds and ends that I may need because I could obtain it at a discount there. Then I started to shop for
the family. For Mrs. Klein I bought a bottle of Chanel, for Hymie, a tie
tack. I went into a music store to buy a Jewish record for Mrs. Klein.
Altogether they had only a few and I could not be certain that she did
not already have those ones. I was supposed to buy some cold cuts and
cocoa for Helga but otherwise I was free until 5:30, at which time I was*

to meet Helga. It was around 4:00. I thought I might like to listen to some records. I listened to Hungarian Rhapsody No. 1 by Liszt, which I ended up buying for Mrs. Klein instead of the Jewish record. They also had the New World Symphony by Dvořák but in an album, which cost seven dollars. I found the price too high, but I listened to the record nevertheless. When I came out of the store, it was exactly 5:30 and I had no time to buy the stuff for Helga. I think she must have been very angry, but in the end we managed to buy what she wanted.

Later on, Albert, the Torontonian, phoned to ask if I would go with him for a car ride. I said, okay. This is the approximate conversation that took place between us. "You know, you are very pretty." "You needn't flatter me. Besides, there is nothing you can tell me I don't already know." "You are very desirable." "Oh, you think so." "Would you slap me if I kissed you?" "I guess I would."

The difference between this and the real conversation is that he appeared really shy in spite of the forward things he said. I did not slap him when he kissed me. I guess I was feeling a little more sentimental than usual. Also I think I liked him, and we did have a very good time talking to each other. At least there will be somebody I know in Toronto. I think that's important too.

The next day, Mr. Klein phoned and told me to take the bus, as Mrs. Hardin would be there to give me a lift. So I phoned to say goodbye to everyone and I took my bike to the Weslers'. By the way, I wonder if they will send it on to me. It was a birthday present, after all.

Fanny and Helga came to the bus station with me to say goodbye. Fanny gave me a blouse she had, which I liked so much. I know it is really awful of me to even think this, but I thought that she might [give it to me].

When I arrived in Vegreville I gave everyone the presents I bought for them. They seemed very pleased but said I shouldn't have spent so much money. Maybe they are right — I have only four dollars left to my name. Later in the evening they [the Kleins] *showed me the letter* [from Congress]. *No chance of going to school. As soon as I get there I will have to start working in a factory. I was so staggered by this news, as if I literally received a great punch in the gut and it almost knocked me out. For a short while it drained me of all my strength. I felt it was the end. How I needed someone to help me and give me some strength of mind! But gradually I strengthened myself. I must have faith in myself. There is no one else I can count on or lean on.*

Yesterday I went everywhere to say my goodbyes here. I found this a most unpleasant task, the hardest of tasks. After that I packed. Including my typewriter, I have six pieces of luggage, substantially more than I arrived with. In the evening, the Hardins and the Tunises came over and gave me ten dollars in an envelope as a parting gift. So did the Kleins, and they also gave me a lovely bracelet, and from Hymie, a box of chocolates. Mrs. Klein said that though at times she may have told me things that hurt me, she loved me very much and everyone loved me. She was crying all day yesterday in advance. She was recalling the day a year ago, how much happier a mood they were in, on the day they went to fetch me.

When I was boarding the train, I was crying sincerely. "I wish I could say all I want," I said. "Thank you." How could they understand how I felt? I couldn't properly explain it.

After all, I spent a year in this awful village. Aside from the Kleins being very good to me, my intuition tells me that my year spent here will cost me in the long run. But in spite of that, I love them. I stood by the window of the train for as long as they were visible to me, until they disappeared from my view.

1949-1950

Leaving Vegreville

On the train, I had a sleeper. I was awakened early by a baby's cry. I was just about to fall back to sleep when the porter very politely came to awaken me.

I had also gone to say goodbye to Mr. Finlay. He told me, like everyone else, that by all means, I should continue with school. He said he was sure that if I stayed in school I would be an honour student every year.

It's ridiculous that people don't even know how to shake hands properly here. They bend their elbow and they act as if they don't want to dirty their own hands, or maybe they think that mine is an Easter egg.

The train stopped for an hour in Saskatoon. I got off, as I wanted to look around a bit. Also I wanted to buy film for my camera. I went into a coffee shop for a glass of orange juice. I didn't have my watch because I didn't get to have it fixed, so I didn't know what time it was. I thought the train was leaving at 1:00. A clock I saw on the street read 1:30. When I asked someone the time, they confirmed that it was 1:30. I got very anxious thinking that the train had left without me. I started running and ran into a policeman. He assured me it was only 12:30. So then, I walked around for another half hour before I got back on the train.

In Regina, an older lady got on the train and took the seat across from me. When the Black porter came to make the bed I sat next to her and we were chatting. She told me she had spent her holiday in the west and was now returning to Toronto. I also got acquainted with a girl who was going to Toronto to study music, I think at the same school where Albert is studying.

Later, the older lady asked me to go with her to the dining car to have a cocoa. In the diner, the waiter said that I would do him a favour by having a piece of raisin pie. It turned out that the lady is his French teacher. She told me her father is a minister. Later on, she gave me a bag of candy. The next morning the waiter brought me a glass of orange juice. The lady gave me her address saying to call her if I had any problems. In my eyes, she will always remain golden-hearted.

September 2

When I arrived in Winnipeg Miss Tessler [a social worker]*, who was very friendly, was waiting for me. She brought me to a place where the people were also very friendly. I will probably stay here* [at the Globermans] *for a few days until they* [the Congress] *correspond with Toronto. Mrs. Globerman and I were talking and it turned out that Esther, the girl I met in Calgary, had stayed with them previously. I remembered that Esther spoke well of the Globermans.*

Miss Tessler said that she is under the impression that I want to go to Toronto on account of Stephen. She said that Gizi Weisz is staying with a family where she helps out while she is going to school. I asked if she could arrange a similar situation for me, as I wanted to go to school under any circumstance. She said she didn't know if she could arrange that for me in Toronto. Otherwise it is only possible to go to school if one could be in a private home; or, if one is exceptional, the Congress pays. Then I was brave enough to tell her that I didn't do badly in school. I had to show her my report card. She wrote down the marks and left.

I phoned Gizi. She was so surprised that for a moment, she was speechless. We arranged for her to visit me this afternoon. I was sitting on pins and needles. I haven't seen a face from home since I left Budapest. She is still as beautiful as when I last saw her. At first Mrs. Globerman kept on talking. Unfortunately, she is the type who, when she gets started, can't stop. Gizi kept looking at her watch but she didn't take the hint. It took over half an hour to free ourselves of her. We went for a walk. She told me she is staying with a family where she is helping out. She has a boyfriend. They understand each other perfectly and, just between themselves, they are engaged. He is twenty and has one more year of university. After that they plan to marry and go to the Eretz [Israel]. Gizi is a true and faithful Shomer [faithful to the beliefs of Hashomer Hatzair].

The next afternoon, Mrs. Globerman, my landlady, asked if I wanted to speak to a Hungarian boy. I said I did. She just happened to be phoning the place where that boy was staying. It turned out that she wanted to arrange a date. At first I thought that this boy was Gabi Kerenyi, someone I knew from the Shomers [Hashomer Hatzair]. *At one time, he had asked me to be his girlfriend. This person said his name was Gabi. I said, "Szervusz* [Hello], *this is Zsuzsi Löffler speaking." "I've never heard of you, my angel," said he. "Aren't you Gabi Kerenyi?" I asked. I was getting pretty annoyed at his impertinent manner. He started asking the usual questions, such as where am I from and do I have a boyfriend. Then he enlightened me that he had a girlfriend. Also he said that every boy had one, but that not all the girls had boyfriends because there was a boy shortage. Finally we agreed that he and his friends would come and visit me the next afternoon at 2:00.*

After that telephone conversation I was certain that he was a conceited and cynical fellow. But when I actually met him, even those qualities I assigned to him were too good. I have never met such an idiotic character.

In the evening I went to visit Gizi. We talked and talked and I ended up staying quite late. She is a smart girl. I think we will be good friends.

The next afternoon, a bunch of Hungarian boys came over. Gabi Kerenyi, Gyuri Mach and others. Also a Canadian girl. Her poor head didn't understand a single word we said. We went for a walk in the park, after which the others dispersed. At 4:00 Gyuri Mach, his girl-friend, and Gabi and I went to the girl's house where her mother made lecsó *for us.*[20] *I didn't admit that I had never eaten* lecsó *in my life because I don't like it. But I tasted it. Gabi walked me home. He came in and we were talking. Then Gizi came over. Gabi left and Gizi and I went back to her place because she had to be home.*

September 4

At 11:00 in the morning, my suitcases arrived. Later Gizi came over and we were exchanging some clothes. It would be rare to find such an impudent little girl as the one here [the daughter of the Globermans]. *She forced me to open* [my suitcase] *and show her my typewriter. But in some sort of a cunning way. After banging away on it for a while, she announced that she had enough of it for now. Now, when I returned home, I found the typewriter open.*[21]

Last night I had a strange dream. I had children whom I was sup-posed to protect. Awake, I never felt such love as I did in this dream.

Gabi phoned around 12:00 to say that he is at his piano teacher's, who would be willing to have me stay at her place if I am interested. I hesitated. "I want to go to Toronto." Gabi was insistent that I should just go and see for myself. He came for me at 3:00.

A very tiny but infinitely charming woman is the person [he told me about]. *After a conversation, she* [Mrs. Lipkin] *said that she would very much like me to come and live with her. I should make a decision by tomorrow.*

---

20 A traditional Hungarian vegetable stew.

21 Susan was unhappy about the daughter playing with her typewriter because it was the one she had brought with her from Hungary, from her father's business, and she treasured it.

September 1949

Perhaps with this new notebook, I am also starting a new life. Perhaps not forever, but for now, a part that I call the "Toronto Period," is over. Since I arrived in Canada, behind every thought of mine there was a desire to go to Toronto. In Toronto, there was Stephen. There was no one anywhere else. Sometimes this feeling was intense, other times, less so, but it always existed. There was no one else I thought of as highly. No one I met who could replace him. To be honest with myself, maybe I don't love him anymore, but I am clinging to the idea of him because I don't want to admit that, after all, I don't love anybody. No one. I'll make my decision dependent on whether I will be allowed to skip a grade and go to Grade 11. I hope I won't regret my decision.

This morning I bathed, washed my hair and got dressed just as Gizi called. She informed me that she made inquiries about the Lipkins from the family she is living with. The two families are related. They didn't say anything favourable. I will have to work hard, won't be able to go out a lot, and more of the same pleasantries. I replied that this was not my impression of the situation. This was too bad to hear, as I had almost made up my mind about it. I said that first of all, by all means, I am going to call Miss Tessler.

Miss Tessler was very uncertain about it. She advised me not to rush into anything. She said she knew many families who were willing to have me live with them under those circumstances. I said I liked this place and if it was possible, I would like to stay there. The reason for this was that I wanted to go to the same school and the same class as Gizi, who lived in the same area. Miss Tessler said she would speak with Mrs. Lipkin and call me back. Meanwhile Gabi called to inquire whether I had made any decisions. He claimed Mrs. Lipkin told him that if I stayed with them, she would do a lot on my behalf. He didn't mention this to me previously because he didn't want to influence me.

After a short time, Miss Tessler called and said I should go to the Lipkins and try it out. It was left at that. I phoned Mrs. Lipkin, who promised to pick me up at 3:00. Then I wrote a letter home, and then I started to pack feverishly, as I had very little time. I could hardly close the suitcase. Finally, about a half hour late, they arrived. Gabi was with them and came with us and kept me company while I tried to unpack, which is an impossible task. I still haven't finished. I have a very tiny room and there is no room for my things. They promised to put up some shelves. Half my stuff is all over the place and the other half is still in the suitcase.

I got ready, as we were going to a Chinese restaurant for dinner. "You look like a picture," Mrs. Lipkin commented when she saw me dressed up. Maybe she doesn't really mean it. This is the very first time I ever had Chinese food. I found it delicious.

Gabi, Marlene and I had plans to go to a movie afterwards. We went to see The Babe Ruth Story. *I saw it before, in Edmonton, but it is a very good film. The second movie was very bad and we walked out in the middle. We walked Marlene home and then he walked me home. He asked if he could come in. No one was home. We listened to the radio, talked about school and about all sorts of other things. Then he started playing with my hair; then somehow or other, I said that if someone wanted to kiss me, I would slap him. Then he said that if he wanted to kiss a girl it would mean that he loves her and wants more of a relationship. He tried to kiss me but I took his arm off my shoulder. As he was leaving at 10:30, I saw him to the door, and he kissed me. "See, you didn't slap me," he said. "I still can," I said. Then he kissed me again and said, for the fifth time, to make sure I was going to wait for him after school the next day.*

September 6
This morning I made my bed and the boys' beds [Raymond's and Victor's]. Mrs. Lipkin took me to school. I had to go to see the principal, Mr. Reeve, about going to Grade 11. He told us I needed to get permission from the Board of Education. We came home and found out exactly where we had to go. Then we made an appointment for 1:30. I ironed a

few things and then left. I was so excited, as if my life depended on the outcome of this appointment.

I told a man with an expressionless face of my situation and then I showed him my report card. He then said, "You didn't take foreign languages, did you?" "Yes, I did," I said. "Three years Latin and two of German." The man of no expression, on whose face it was impossible to read what he was thinking, listened to me describing my situation and took a piece of paper on which he wrote something with a terrible scrawl. He gave it to me, saying to give it to the principal. He said he would write a letter to him. "Can I go to Grade 11?" I asked. The man-with-no-expression nodded. I was so happy I didn't know what to do with myself.

From there we went to the [Lipkins'] *store* [Adrienne's on Portage Avenue] *and from there I got a lift to school. At school, there was a long lineup. Just as I got to the front of the line, the principal announced that he had no more time* [to meet with students].

On the way out I met up with Gabi. For the first time, I went to the library to register and took out some books. Shaw's Pygmalion *and other plays. I will take out more serious and scholarly books. I know that I don't know much, but I want to learn. We walked home and Gabi said that he would phone. He came over in the evening. The Lip-*kins went out. We listened to records, among others the opera Lucia di Lammermoor.

Even though we have spent quite a bit of time together in the last several days, we don't know each other at all. We are just talking about general things. I am not in love with him. I don't even know if I like him, but I still wanted him to kiss me. He did kiss me when he left.

September 7

I went to school for 9:00. I stood in line for an hour and a half before I got in to see the principal. He is an infinitely charming man. But in spite of this he only wrote down my name and told me to come back the next day and then he will place me in a class.

All afternoon I was ironing. I was not in a happy mood. I spoke with Gizi and she is also down in the dumps. She doesn't like the class she was placed in yesterday and she was talking about quitting school. On account of that her social worker isn't willing to buy her a schoolbag for now. However, she has already changed her mind. Gabi phoned. He has lots of homework. We will meet at school tomorrow.

A horrible accident happened last night during supper. I was bringing a hot cup of coffee to the table; just then Raymond stood up and the cup was pushed out of my hand and the coffee spilled on him. He got very painful burns. Immediately they called his uncle, who is a doctor, who came and bandaged him up. Mr. Lipkin clearly blamed me. I was extremely upset and felt very isolated. I would have liked to complain to someone or cry, but there was no one close by to whom I could complain. Although Mrs. Lipkin came to my defense, it didn't change my mood for the better.

Then I did the dishes and washed and waxed the kitchen floor. I started reading the book I got from the library. Today I finished reading the book Gizi lent me. It was very good.

St. John's Technical High School [Susan's school] *has a uniform for girls — a blue tunic that doesn't even cover the thigh. It barely covers my panties and black stockings. Good God, how will I look in that outfit?*

September 8
Today, I finally got into a class, Room 29. On this occasion, I am unbelievably lucky. Because many students failed last year, some kids will take a double load to complete their year. I was put into that accelerated class so that I will be able to finish Grade 11. Of course, only if I pass. The kids seem very nice. There was some mix up. I am taking Latin while the others are taking something else. I didn't know where my next class was, and I was just standing amid a heaving group of young people and for several minutes I had no idea what to do. But luckily I met up with some boys who were in the same situation as me, and they had a timetable.

After lunch, I stood in line for a long time for books. When I was almost at the door, there was an announcement that we were to come back tomorrow.

Gizi is in the same class as me. I think she isn't so thrilled to have me there. Her future brother-in-law is coming to Winnipeg today, and she is stressed out about that. She is going to her mother-in-law's after school.

Mrs. Lipkin arranged for Gabi to have an exceptionally good piano teacher for free. We had a geometry test. At least half of it I couldn't do. In that [subject] I was the best in Vegreville. How will I do in the rest of the subjects?

Gabi came over. He helped me with the geometry homework. Gizi phoned.

September 18
Saturday morning we went downtown. I got my tunic. Then I met Gabi and we went to see his teacher. He is an exceptionally charming man. He is the conductor of the Winnipeg Symphony Orchestra. His name is Walter Kaufmann (he kissed me on the cheek).

In the evening I went to the Y with Gabi. It is a Jewish club. There were lots of kids there from school. Also I met a few Hungarian kids. I noticed about Gabi, however he tries to deny it, that he still likes his old girlfriend, Marlene. She is a tall, dark, beautiful girl, who, according to him, is dumb. But probably that is an additional sex appeal. I can hardly stand the way he is acting. He is missing something of good manners. On our way home I tried to tell him that I really don't know him, and I hoped we would get to know each other so we could be good friends. But from the beginning, he misunderstood me. He thought I wanted him to say that he likes me.

On Sunday I went to visit a Hungarian girl. But before that, I went to the Globermans for my mail. Stephen wrote and sent a picture. I am longing so much for someone and I realize from his letter how much he is looking forward to my coming, for him. I got a letter from the Kleins as well. According to the letter, they miss me a lot. I am curious what the fate of my bike is. Will they send it?

At Kathy's, the Hungarian girl I had met, I met a Canadian boy. He was crazy about me.[22] He asked for my phone number and he phoned me that day. He asked me out. He immediately wanted to neck and I wasn't willing. Even now, the thought of him makes me nauseous.

At school, troubles are starting. There was a Latin test and I got 2 per cent. The teacher came to talk to me and he said that he just wanted to call my attention to the fact that I am not doing too well, and probably I wouldn't want to fail in June. Perhaps I would be better off not attending the accelerated class. I was very upset, and I asked him to give me permission to try. He said he would give me a week. Since that day, every day I have been studying till 1:00 in the morning. The result was that yesterday he came over and announced that he noticed a great improvement.

Lusia, a girl I met in Calgary, is coming to Winnipeg. I really liked her there. But it seems to me that she doesn't make a good impression on others. That is not the kind of friend I wish for. I have no time to meet with Gizi outside of school, but we spend a lot of time talking on the phone.

I wrote Stephen and asked him if he would consider coming here. It was very difficult for me to write this letter, but, finally, with great difficulty, I sent it. I don't believe he will come. First of all, because when I asked if he would come to Edmonton and he wanted to, I nixed it. Two days ago, I believed that I would be totally happy if he were here. But today, I am so depressed that nothing seems to matter. Now, the way things are, I am just spending time studying and nothing else.

Maybe I miss Gabi coming here in the evenings like he used to. I had asked him to help me with Latin. He did come a couple of times

---

22 This is the first sentence Susan wrote in her diary in English.

and helped. Last year he got 88 per cent. "You won't get that," he said jokingly. "We'll see," I replied. He studied it for six years at home, and he didn't skip doing it for a year like I did, during which time you can forget things. I will be satisfied if I pass.

Mrs. Lipkin is extremely nice. She is very taken with me. I got a few dresses and a suit from them and she will give me one of her fur coats. Therefore I will give my fur coat, which is a little bit big on me anyways, to Helga. She wrote that she could not go to Montreal until December because she wants to buy a fur coat for herself. I hope mine will be good for her. I just hope that the Kleins won't send it on [to someone else]. When I left, it was still in storage.

September 24

Today is Rosh Hashanah. Yesterday I got the suit. It is dark blue and very stylish. And a sweet little red hat. Yesterday, Gabi and the Fishmans — Mrs. Lipkin's sister's family — were here for supper. Tonight, we went to the Fishmans.

Yesterday I had a very good talk with Mrs. Lipkin. She really likes me and has great ambitions for me. It is lucky that her ambitions correspond to mine, such as learning to play the piano, going to university, marrying a doctor and other such pleasantries.

Today I got a reply from Stephen. He would come; nothing holds him to Toronto, but he has to know that he would have work in his field. I will have to make inquiries about that.

I went to synagogue where I met a bunch of Hungarians and half the school was also there. In the afternoon I went to the store to help. I got a pair of gloves.

I received News Year's greetings from Gizi, the Tunises and the Hardins. I had in mind to send some out, too, but I didn't have an opportunity to buy some [cards]. But supposedly, next week is still not too late.

Today I took a few pictures. Mr. Lipkin will teach me how to develop them. That will be my hobby. This interests me a lot. I would like to take pictures of people when they are not aware of it so that they may be very natural and true.

A boy phoned Lusia saying that he would like to get to know her because he heard a lot about her. Lusia has no idea who he is. Today he was going to her place. I am curious. Tonight, I had an argument with Vicky [Victor] and Raymond. I had to show them my stamp collection and had to look at theirs. I received two sets of stamps that were printed on the occasion of the 1949 World Youth Meetings from Bözsi.[23] *I gave one set to Raymond.*

October 8

Someone phoned saying he would like to meet me. I had no idea who he was. I said that if he wants he could come here. He is a disgusting individual, but he took a bunch of photos of me and on account of wanting to get copies of the pictures I was forced to abide his daily calls. Today I went to the movies with him. The joke in this whole story is that he already called for me yesterday, but I was supposed to go with the Lipkins. So I said that someone had already called me to go out and I was going to see Christopher Columbus. *But we ended up not going. He called me again today and I got myself caught up in my own lies by saying that I had seen that movie the day before. But I really did want to see it, and so did he, so I said that I would not mind seeing it again. I was afraid that he would ask me something about it, but in the end I gave myself away by asking whether the movie is in colour. But the idiot didn't notice. I was really in a very low mood, and I amused myself by teasing his poor head.*

Lusia's boy was a no-show.

An encouraging event took place in school. We had a history test of

---

23 The World Assembly of Youth was an international organization founded in 1949 to encourage cooperation, discuss issues and promote relations between youth from all countries that had membership in the United Nations.

which at least half was geography, most of which was not known to me. I was afraid that I didn't pass and I went to speak to the teacher. He said not to worry, I will pick it up, and that I did all right. Mr. Finlay, the principal and my homeroom teacher from Vegreville, had to write whether he recommended for me to be in the accelerated class. He wrote that he believes that I am "exceptionally clever." I was at the top of the class in algebra and geometry. To be sure, this year, I won't be. Even here, there was an article about me in the paper. People are so boring. This is what I think.

I received letters from Zsuzsi Lausch, Aniko [Schonfeld], Panni Sos, and Csoppi Schwartz. Zsuzsi wrote such a sweet letter, as if we have not been so far away from each other for such a long time. With the others, it seems that they are just performing a long-postponed duty. Fabian and Zsuzsi Löwy wrote also.

Hopefully, Stephen's case is also being arranged toward a good conclusion. The manager of one firm, Birks, is going to Toronto. He will look Stephen up and if he finds him satisfactory, he will be hired. Esther [Mrs. Lipkin] is not very happy regarding this matter. According to her, I will marry Stephen and all her plans will collapse. In vain I tried to explain that at no time did I have such, or a similar, plan; she didn't believe me.

Gizi is sick. Yesterday I went to visit her and we had a very good talk.

A few days ago Gabi's mother arrived in Canada.

October 9
Gabi was here for dinner tonight. I am asking myself whether or not it is just sour grapes,[24] but now I find him very unappealing. He is not at all good-looking. Interesting that I actually never "looked" at him. Maybe because I didn't want to feel disillusioned. I didn't lose anything.

---

24 Being critical of something because you cannot have it.

Lusia was here and partly we were studying, partly messing around.

There was a party here once. A very cute boy [Morley Silver] *had come here to say that his mother couldn't make it. Esther introduced us but we never spoke to one another. Today he called and asked if I would go with him to a premiere. He is in the movie business and he is allowed to bring a guest to this premiere. He is twenty years old and seems to be a pleasant conversationalist.*

After supper I went to visit Lusia and stayed till 11:00. When I came home, Esther was teaching me proper English pronunciation. She made me repeat a word twenty times. The more English I learn, I realize how little I know.

Today Miss Tessler phoned to say that the Kleins phoned the Congress asking whether they should send me the bike. Why the Congress and not me, I wonder?[25] *But the main thing is that they should send it.*

October

School is giving me a terrible headache. All the teachers tell us, "If you were foolish enough to go to the accelerated class, then you have to study hard. We are expecting a lot more from you than from the other class." It is allowed to expect, the rest we shall see, I tell myself. I will need some luck to pass the October tests.

Morley phoned to ask if I could go with him to the premiere.

Today there was a tea here. As usual, I was horribly bored, but according to Esther, "I lit up the room." Though, that was actually really needed as there was a short-circuit for a while. Candles were lit for the company. Esther says everyone is impressed with me. They think I am beautiful and are jealous of her because of me. "What should I say then," I said. "I hope you, too, are satisfied," she replied.

We spoke of Ellen [Gizi Weisz, now Ellen Wise] *and her plans of getting married shortly. In connection with this I said that mutual*

---

25 Susan wrote the expression "I wonder" in English.

respect between marriage partners is the most important. I want to feel proud of him; he should be stronger and smarter than me so that he may be my support and protection. Will this come true, I wonder?

The last few nights I have been having this dream that either Mother or Father will die. At times, the actual scene is repeated in my dream, and I know that they will not return. And in my dream I cry so, as I never did when awake. And my heart aches so much, more than when I am awake. In other dreams, I love somebody. In my dream I love so much, more than I have ever loved someone when I am awake. Why do such feelings break out while I sleep?

We had to write a composition in history. "Thought and imagination good," wrote the teacher on it. I used to get As.

October 11
I spent the day studying to make the remains of yesterday's tea [party] *disappear. Later Lusia came over and helped to put things away. Then we went to her place.*

In the meantime, Morley phoned saying that the premiere was postponed, but if I wanted, we could go to a movie. He came for me at 8:00. We were conversing for a while, then we went to see The Great Sinner *with Gregory Peck and Ava Gardner. It was very good. After, we went to a place for ice cream. We were talking for a while; then he brought me home. He is nice.*

November 1
Since last time, Morley phoned and asked if I wanted him to come here and help me with my studies. I said, no, I can do it all by myself. This belongs among my imbecilic things. After we saw each other, I liked him; I liked him a lot. Esther said that she met Morley, who related that a whole bunch of boys who saw us together inquired about who I was, but he wouldn't give out my phone number. And how he is impressed with my beautiful eyes. I like him, too, but God forbid that I should appear

to grab every opportunity to see him. So I told him that I didn't need his help. But now it doesn't matter at all.

I got a letter from Stephen. He asks whether I really don't have a boyfriend and says I should try to get a place [for him] near where I live. My conscience is really bothering me on account of him. I haven't seen him for so long that I don't think that now I like him as a boy, but more like a friend. I had lots of time to think and analyze every little thing that he told me. Is he not looking for a girl who could mother him and be supportive of him? I don't even know why these thoughts are in my head. For, surely, I clearly remember that when we were together, I thought the exact opposite; I thought that he was strong and I would be able to lean on him. I have no cause for pangs of conscience! Really, everything depends on him. I want to love him.

Last night I dreamt about Sali [Pali Salamon]. Interesting, at home I didn't want him and now I often think how silly I was. He is a very handsome and intelligent boy, but I didn't like him. Once I went with Zsuzsi Lausch to a Hanhac miha *[Hanoar Hatzioni children's home] and that's when I met him for the first time. Later on, I heard rumours that he liked Zsuzsi. Next we met at a school ball. He often asked me to dance, but then he said there was no point in asking me because after only a couple of steps, someone else came and asked me.*

Then he asked me to go with him to a program and dance that was taking place at school. Aniko [Schonfeld] happened to be standing with us and I invited her along. This may seem strange, but I thought that he was just asking me as a friend, as it was Zsuzsi who he liked. When we got home from the program I told Aniko that "I could like this boy if I thought he liked me."

Next he asked me to go on a bike excursion. That's when I got to know the "gang," his friends. There were several boys and I was the only girl. We biked to Visegrád.[26] We didn't want to return riding our bikes, because none of us could sit anymore. Each of us put in all the money

---

26 A small castle town about forty kilometres north of Budapest.

we had and with great difficulty, we managed to have enough money to come home by boat.

Then, the seventh gimnázium class, where he was going, was putting on a play. Sali was the director. Zsuzsi Lausch and I were asked to participate. The title of the play was Rifle. It was a very good play. In the end, at the very last minute, it was not performed because the father of one little boy actor didn't give him permission to participate.

In the meantime, me, Zsuzsi Lausch and the "gang" got together often. We went on excursions, to the theatre, to movies. I knew by then that he liked me, but I didn't like him. But I was impressed when Zsuzsi would tell me how he spoke about me, among other things, "Doesn't she look like a little angel?" You can't imagine how much he loves you, Zsuzsi kept telling me. In spite of myself, I was playing with him. Once, I said that I didn't want to go out with him. And then when he didn't call me, I changed my mind. Because I didn't want to throw away someone who loved me I would convince myself that I did love him. And this went on for a while until I finally told him that I didn't love him like a boyfriend and let's be friends. He replied, "You are too beautiful for a boy to just think of you as a friend."

When I was leaving for Canada, I wanted to say goodbye to him and to the rest of the gang. I didn't find him at home. I found another one of the boys, Gyuri Engel. Gyuri said he would like to meet with me and talk to me before I left. He was the one who always kept telling me what a nice boy Sali is, and I would go out with him [Gyuri] and I would meet him sometimes, too. He [Gyuri] is a very intelligent boy and I liked to listen to him talk. I liked him purely as a friend. Among other things, he expressed the view that he doesn't believe in marriage and in love. Therefore I was totally floored that when we met, he declared his love for me and he said that he knew and believed that I loved him too and I shouldn't go to Canada. When he saw that he couldn't convince me of that, he said that I should tell him whether I love him and if I do, he would do everything in his power to come too. I am sorry, I said, maybe I loved somebody for the first time in my life, but it wasn't him.

Thinking back, I really liked the whole bunch of them, and I would like to know what they are all doing, what happened to them. But they probably feel I offended them, especially their hearts. I will write Zsuzsi Lausch and I will find out about them from her.[27]

School is all right. So far I passed everything. I still don't know about the English test. On the other hand, Lusia failed all her subjects except physics. I feel very bad for her, and also I know I would feel lost without her in class.

Something very silly or unpleasant happened. Though in reality it has no effect on me, it is still unpleasant. I mentioned to Esther that I wouldn't go out again with a certain boy. She ran into another boy, who said he wanted to ask me out. Esther, who thought this was the first boy, told him not to bother because I have a date.

With others, when someone dies, in time the pain subsides. With me it is the opposite. As time passes for me it is more painful as I realize more and more what I have lost. I despise myself for the times they [Susan's parents] *may have quarrelled on my account or when I caused them moments of discomfort. I remember little things, which were signs of the deep love they had for me, the kind that perhaps no one, ever again, will feel toward me. Photographs of me displayed saying "Our Susan." My father would rub my stockings before putting them on me so they would be soft on my feet and shouldn't hurt me. My mother would take my feet and put my socks and shoes on* [to keep them warm] *before waking me to get me out of bed. When, once, I was very ill, my father said that he wouldn't wish to live if something happened to me. When I was eight years old, I started writing a book. I remember him reading parts of it out loud. He was so proud of me. He helped me study and both of them wanted so much for me to go to the gimnázium and be a good student. Why can't they see it now,* [and be] *happy, when finally I could make them proud of me? Why can't they be here*

---

27 Susan wondered if they felt that she led them on. When Susan met Zsuzsi (Suzie) many years later, Zsuzsi didn't remember "the gang."

with me now? I would like to throw myself on the ground and scream hysterically, but I can't. Indeed, I have to put on a sweet face because I cannot let on what I truly am. Who would keep me if they knew how wicked I really am. But I will show them that in spite of it all I will get all I want and reach my goal. I will show them, and then I won't care less what anybody thinks.

December 24[28]
About a month ago, Morley took me out again. I didn't have an espe-cially wonderful time, but I felt good about it. I think he is very good-looking. There is something gentle about him. He dances gracefully. He is very courteous. I like all these things about him. We went to the drug-store and had ice cream. When we were standing at the door he kissed me, very lightly and softly, and only for an instant. Then he left. He has very warm and soft lips. For many days afterwards I felt a wonderful thrill at remembering it. It is not a very exciting feeling; it isn't painful and I didn't miss him. It just felt good and easy.

The next day Esther mentioned that she spoke with Mrs. Silver and this is what she said to her. "I don't know what it is with Morley. He takes out other girls too, but he says nothing about them. When he takes out Susan, he comes home and keeps talking about how nice she is."

After this, Morley phoned me and we were speaking on the phone for quite a while. But then I said that I was very busy and I had study-ing to do. He didn't ask to take me out. I was supposed to be studying for my Christmas exam, but I didn't feel like it. I guess I wasn't in the mood.

January 8, 1950
Gabriel's [Gabi's] mother arrived in Winnipeg. She is living with us. It was to be only for a few days but it stretched into a month. It also pre-vented me from studying. Gabriel and George [his first cousin] were

---

28 Susan's first entry in English. The subsequent entries were written in Hungarian up until April 1950, at which point Susan began to write solely in English.

here every night. At first George came only to visit her. I asked him if he had a girlfriend. He said he didn't; he just goes to the movies sometimes with his friends. I said, "Why don't you take a girl to the movies? It would be much more interesting." Next time he came, he asked me to go to the movies with him. When we came home I asked if he wanted to come in and listen to records I just bought. We danced and talked.

The next day he came and asked me if I wanted to go steady with him. I tried to be smart enough not to say yes and not to say no and still satisfy him. I succeeded.

On Sunday when George was angry with me, I went to the midnight show with another Hungarian George and Tibor, two Hungarian refugee boys. Tibor brought me home and wanted to kiss me; what a fool. I really had to fight with him to make him leave me alone. But I was lucky because Esther and Dave [Mr. Lipkin] got in just before us. I just laughed at him. "I lost that one," he said.

Then school started. I couldn't settle down at all. The first week I was absent more than I was present. This is something I never dared to do in all my life. I remember, once, when I did it at home, but I was even afraid to go out on the street because my conscience bothered me so much.

I had one pleasant surprise, though. I got 76 per cent on my Latin test, which I was sure I had failed. I just passed algebra and geometry. Lusia got 2 per cent in the latter. But in physics I got an awful mark, 32 per cent. Lusia got 27 per cent.

January 9

We organized a club in the Pioneer Women.[29] We want to have several activities. I am the vice-president. Yesterday we had a meeting and made plans to have a tea. It will be in the near future.

---

29 A group founded in the United States in 1925 as part of the Labor Zionist movement. It is now known as Na'amat, a term based on a Hebrew acronym that means "Movement of Working Women and Volunteers."

We went to visit Gabriel's mother, who was working as a nurse with a family for a few days. Gabriel was there and then he came home with us. Then he went with Marlene to visit George's mother in the hospital. Then Gabriel, Marlene and George came over. Marlene sat down and was reading comics. She didn't want to dance, and she didn't want to do anything except go home. I was so fed up with them that as they were leaving I said, "It was nice to have you." I would be a darned fool to have her here again. I think she never wants to come over, and she doesn't even want us to go there. "I want Gabriel to come over," she said, when I called her to come to the party. And Gabriel wanted to come. Even if she is a beautiful girl, it must be boring to be with her all the time. After about ten minutes, she phoned to say she was sorry. Probably Gabriel made her because he wanted to stay. George stayed and we were talking until about 11:00. Then I told George that he had to leave as I still had to bathe and wash my hair. I also wanted to catch up on my writing here. I told him I didn't want him to come over on weekdays. But I am afraid that if he doesn't come, I will miss, not him particularly, but I will be lonely in the evening. I didn't get to bed until after 2:00. Of course, today I feel like a dog. I couldn't do much studying either, but luckily I don't have much homework yet.

At lunchtime at school today, Lusia, Ellen and I were discussing free love. In the end we all agreed to be against it. I hope Ellen will soon be engaged.

January 11

Yesterday George was here. Just when I thought he liked me the most, I told him that I am sure he doesn't love me and I don't love anyone either. I want him not to want me to be his steady girlfriend, just simply friends. He made me explain this to him very thoroughly and seemed not to understand. I know it was very mean of me. It was very unfair that I kissed him first and then I said what I said. But anyway, now it is done.

February 2

Somehow everything seems to me to be in a different colour than two months ago. Then, I thought I was as well off as possible, nothing more I need to expect from life. Now, again, I am very dissatisfied and troubled. Who is doing me any favours and why do I need to be grateful? Why? I am beginning to perceive people and life. No matter what anyone does, in front of their eyes is their own self-interest. Why, Esther? She puts herself in such a light as if she were the best creature on earth, a do-gooder for everyone. I am the one who stays at home with her misbehaving brats so she can go out and enjoy herself. I am her daughter?! If I were, I would be going out, not her. All right, I am not her daughter. But lately she tells me — too often — how fantastic it is for me [with her], what an angel she is, and how everyone ought to be envious of my good luck! I am living a rotten life — I sit at home six evenings a week, on Saturdays I go to help out in the store [Adrienne's], on Sundays I clean the house, and in the afternoons I attend a stinking meeting because I owe her that for her renown. And I am supposed to be grateful to fate, or better said, to her? She is good on the outside. She gave me a dress so people can see how beautifully she dresses me. And it is true that sometimes we have good talks, but lately, more often than not, I cannot stand her.

For example, on Thursday I went to a dance. I had a great time. Really very good. Three boys asked to take me home. Also a lady asked me if I would be willing to have my picture taken for the newspaper. Then I felt really happy, and something has to happen to spoil it for me.

Yesterday, from suppertime till 1:00 I worked. Not slowly and comfortably but very hard. By chance, Lusia was here and she helped me. I washed the kitchen furniture and everything, only that I should force her [Esther] to say that she is satisfied with what I do at home. Not only was she not satisfied, but she didn't even notice. Darn it anyways! What's the point in even trying? I am not going to keep the kitchen clean for myself.

This morning at 10:00 I had to go somewhere to have a picture taken

*of me for the newspaper. (I am to present a cheque to someone.) The
lady phoned and said that the photographer may be a bit late and asked
me to wait for him. Esther started to get upset with me when I, unsus-
pecting, told her this. She said that the store will be busy and how do I
imagine that I could wait. And sometimes she is so insolently cunning.
She asked if I am going to Frank's party. (I shouldn't forget Kati [Kathy]
is moving in, which I am very happy about.) I said that I wasn't because
I am going somewhere else. She said, "Who said you are? Who gave you
permission? You were already out on Thursday." The blood rushed to
my head. Until now I used to go out on Saturdays and no other time.
On a few occasions, I dared to ask and she was forced to spend an
evening at home. I shouldn't dare to think that I got one extra night out.*

*Is it possible that I will live like this until I get married? I will cer-
tainly have to do something so that this won't happen. The problem is I
am too mixed up with them now. Why do I always get myself into such
situations?*

*There is a boy at school, Lusia's old love, who is staring at me. But
so persistently that it is really embarrassing. It seems as if everyone [at
school] is trying to be friendly but we don't know how to allow ourselves to be approached, perhaps because we want it too much.*

*I dreamt that I was waiting for news about my father. I was so ter-
ribly afraid. I was suffering and fearing so. Then I heard that he was
dead. Oh, I don't know, I can't write about it. It hurts so. It still does.
There was an aching, biting feeling in my heart. I felt so much alone and
lonely. Why do I have to dream such things? I hate my life and hate myself sometimes. Would it not be easier to be where they are? Or should I
condemn myself for feeling sorry for myself?*

April 15

*I spent the first few mornings of the holiday [Passover, April 2–8] at
home. One day I cleaned and another day I waxed three rooms. Toward
the end I felt I couldn't do any more, I was so tired. I worked so that I
put all my energy into it. Perhaps now Esther will notice that I am try-*

ing to do something to please her (which according to her, I don't do). She phoned in the afternoon to ask what I was doing. When I told her she said, "Didn't you do that yesterday?" When I got ready I went to the store. The next day she was shouting about why hadn't I given Vicky socks. That's why she is leaving me at home, not to wax floors. Whatever a person is doing, she has a way of making nothing of it and even turns it around to make something bad of it.[30]

On Sunday George phoned and asked if I wanted to go to the Y. I haven't been to a dance in a long time and I really wanted to go. Kathy and I went and we had a very good time. We were dancing the whole time. When it was over we got this idea to go to a tea-leaves reader. Some of the boys who wanted to walk us home got scared off by this idea. But one very courageous one was willing to come with us. But we did give up tea-leaves reading for that night. Instead we went to the drugstore for a bite to eat. The boy asked for my telephone number. I really don't care if he calls or not.

Monty, a boy who once took me home from the Habonim, called me. Yesterday I went with him to a party. The crowd was very nice and friendly. It was quite nice; I was having a good time but nothing special. Something was missing. I could never care for Monty as a boyfriend. I didn't get a thrill out of it with my whole heart full of it, feeling like I didn't want it to end.

On Thursday I had a concert ticket with [illegible]. We were to meet on the corner of Main and Selkirk. I was in the store so I was in a rush to get there on time. I was running and, unfortunately, fell. I got up and continued running. Later I noticed that my whole foot, dress and even overshoes were full of blood. Another ruined stocking and a mangled foot for a while. We heard "The Creation" by Haydn. I really, really liked it. I know practically nothing about music, but I do enjoy listening to it. I will go as often as my time and money will permit me to.

---

30 From this point on Susan's diary was written is English.

The same day, Gabriel, Olga and Anna were here. Gabriel was very proud of himself because he got 62 per cent in literature, the highest in his room. He is such a selfish and self-centred person that I don't envy any girl who will fall in love with him.

Monty took a picture of me at the party and promised to bring me a copy. I am curious to see it.

I was reading a lot during the holidays, too. Shaw's Pygmalion, *Thomas Mann's* The Transposed Heads, *Rachel Field's* All This and Heaven Too. *I liked this book so much I could hardly put it down. But I had to be at the store. I helped make a certain kind of bra with a zipper in the front. It was Esther's idea. It is selling very fast. Most probably it will be a very good business for them.*

April 18
On Sunday afternoon I took my bike and went for a ride. In the meantime I went to visit Anna and Olga. They said Hungary had declared an amnesty and that until September we could go home.[31] Sometimes, maybe not seriously, I consider the matter. Then Kathy and I were taking pictures. In the evening we went to a costume ball. A boy had called me earlier and asked to take me but I told him I didn't have a costume. There was that crazy little Anton. He took me home and said that if I wanted to go to Toronto he would get an apartment for me. He must have something wrong with his head if he thinks that I will be his mistress or, worse, his wife. Kathy asked me to go around with him, at least for a while, because she thinks then Anton wouldn't go [to Toronto] *and Frank wouldn't go without Anton. I'd like to help her but I get*

31 The Communist government considered people who had left Hungary as having abandoned their country, and refugees believed they would face repercussions — such as arrest — if they returned. Susan believed that it was safe for her to return at this point because there was a general impression that the situation had changed and that the Communist government would not persecute those who had left as refugees.

nauseated even by looking at him. Yesterday he came over with Frank, and against my own will, I was compelled to leave the room, excusing myself by saying I had studying to do. He asked me why I didn't go with him to the Playhouse [a theatre]. *I replied that I didn't want to go with him. He can think whatever he likes.*

I know four of my marks already. I got 73 per cent in Latin, 60 per cent in math, 56 per cent in general science and chemistry combined, and 58 per cent in history. Lusia, poor thing, failed three. She went low down to 19 in math, 33 in science, 40s in German. Gabriel, of course, tops everybody. He got in the 90s in most subjects.

May 4

Quite a long time ago I heard that now everybody is allowed to go back to Hungary. I didn't give much thought to the matter then. But later on when Esther caused me a few bitter hours, the thought started growing in my head. Then I got letters from both Ilus and Malvin asking me to come home. Then, I started to consider it seriously. What if I stay here? What if I go home? If I stay, most probably I will have to struggle a little bit, I will be somebody's slave a little bit. At best I marry a rich Canadian boy. I could have a house and let us say a car. So what? Would that make my life happy? If I go home I would have my family, my friends, and may even have more opportunities than here. The more I thought of it, the more I was deciding in favour of going home. When I became convinced that this was what I really wanted, I felt happy. It is peculiar that maybe for the first time I was happy at the thought of going home.

Yesterday I went to see Mr. Nemeth, who holds some kind of position with the Hungarian Kossuth club [Hungarian-Canadian club] *to ask him to help me arrange this matter. He told me I didn't have to worry about travelling expenses because the Hungarian government will pay for it and many opportunities will be available to me. He said that here there will be a depression in two years and then nobody will even have enough to eat. Today I wrote a letter to the Hungarian consulate inquiring about the matter. It will take a while probably but I want to finish the school year anyway and work for a while because I want to have a lot of things.*

Monty brought me the picture from the party. I went to the movies with him a couple of times, but I really can't stand him. According to Esther, he is handsome and adorable. According to Kathy, he is nice and she advises me to go out with him. But he is málészájú.[32]

May 5

Today is Ellen's wedding. I am really very, very happy for her. Shieky [nickname for Ellen's husband, Yehoshua Brownstone] is a lovely boy. He is intelligent and he loves her. I am sure they will be very happy. Only Judy and I are invited from among the refugees.

It was raining badly and I arrived at the last minute for the pictures. Ellen looked lovely in a white bridal gown. And Shieky, too. Everything was very nice. It is really wonderful to see a couple who loves each other so much. I gave her a handiwork that Malvin sent me last Christmas. I didn't have a single cent and I simply had to give her something.

Today, all day, I felt terrible. Maybe it was the influence of the wedding. I want somebody to want me. Everything seems so empty. I dread the thought of doing the dishes, cleaning up and going to the store. I wish I were home already.

It still seems impossible to me that Ellen is married. I think of Ellen at home, who was going around with little boys, fatally in love with them. Ellen is now a woman, who was already not a girl, in these last days. She told me that and I think they are very brave and smart. Why wait when they know they are getting married? Why spend their wedding day in intense excitement and fear instead of enjoying themselves? I don't think that those things are forbidden and dreadful, but necessity and enjoyment.

---

32 A Hungarian word meaning clumsy, sheep-faced or someone who always has their mouth open.

What a dreadful, miserable day! The rain is just pouring and the whole neighborhood is flooded. How nice it would be to get into bed with a good book without any worry and responsibility, or better, sleep as much as you want. I haven't been able to do that for so long. But, well, let us hope everything turns out for the best and hope we will have a little bit of a blue sky and sunshine in this stormy, thunderous sky.

Lusia is moving to another place. I hope soon she will be able to join her mother in New York. Until then, I am sure she will not be happy. Today I sent letters to the Hungarian consulate and to the Kleins. I wonder what each will answer. I will also write to my dear relatives, the Kleins, in New York.[33]

May 7

Yesterday, when the family came home, Kathy declared to me that she is moving from here. Lately, she has not been feeling well. She went to see her doctor who said that she is suspicious of T.B. [tuberculosis]. After several examinations it was discovered that she had T.B. quite a while ago but she hasn't got it now, though she has inactive germs and she has to be very careful. Esther became very anxious and worried that any of us might get it. She didn't let her in at home and later she [Kathy] had to have a separate plate. Kathy wanted to leave anyways and this was just another reason. She made the doctor say that she needed rest and has to be in a quiet house. She is moving tomorrow. I will miss her.

The river is rising and houses are flooded already. At the riverbank, houses are standing half in water. The expectation is that it will keep rising.

May 8

Kathy didn't sleep at home today. She moved to Norma's, where she lived before, but her clothes are still here. There she will pay sixteen

---

33 The family of Susan's paternal great-uncle.

dollars a month for rent and she will cook for herself and Frank. I think she is a big fool. He always loves her when he can use her. He doesn't work now and has no money. Without any pangs of conscience, he eats her food, takes her money and even lets her take him out. I do not like this business. I tell her at every chance I get, because she asks me, and she knows it. But when the chance comes again, she always has excuses for him. But, well, that's love, I guess. And surely he is a good-looking boy.

Today, after I cleaned up, I wanted to go out for a bike ride and look around and see what the flood situation looked like. Gabriel came over and I went with him to George's. They live near the Red River on the other side. We could hardly get across the bridge, the traffic was so great. Only residents and workers have the right to go. George's house is in the water. Lots of sandbags are on the side of it to prevent the water from getting to it. When we got there, they were still working. People are not even allowed to walk on one side of the street. Then they were going to Marlene's, where I didn't want to go. Olga said I shouldn't because they are jealous of me. I really do not know why; they surely have no reason at all, but after this I suppose they do not like me very much. At Luxton [a neighbourhood], people are sailing in the streets. Then I went to Lusia's. She just moved today. She now lives right next door to Ellen. She spoke to her on the phone, but Ellen was busy as they are leaving for their honeymoon tomorrow. A little later I went there, but she wasn't at home. Then Lusia and I went to Kathy's. Then I walked Lusia home and I was going home. On the way, I saw a bunch of boys sitting in front of a house. As I was passing by, one of them called to me in Hungarian. It was Benny, a boy I met at Kathy's party. He asked me out but I said I was busy. I didn't even like him but Kathy was telling me many nice things about him. Therefore, when he said he would call me I said okay.

At home, Esther told me that my social worker, Miss Mindess, phoned me. Really, she said that she wanted to give me five dollars for my examination, but I sensed something else behind it. I know that *she knows I want to go home. So Esther tells me, "Miss Mindess wants you to pick up the money on Monday, at her place. You will meet her sister and her brother and his friends." The matter seems to me very suspicious. Mostly because, according to Esther's notion, if I fall in love, I wouldn't want to go home. I promised her I won't [go home] but she also promised me she will do everything in her power that I should [fall in love]. Now what have Miss Mindess's brother and his friends got to do with me? Although Lusia met him in the office once and said he is very nice to talk to.*

By the way, I met Monty on Saturday. He said they were flooded, too. He will buy tickets for the circus, which just came to town. I am not too happy for two reasons: 1. I will be with him. 2. I'd rather go to a movie than to the circus. But what can you do?

So back to the other story. I asked Esther what all this was about. She said innocently, "What are you talking about?" But I knew she had said something that I didn't like. But she denied it. At last, Kathy told me that she had this idea, which she communicated to Miss Mindess, that if I fell in love, I wouldn't go. Now with joined aims, they want me to fall in love. Well, I rebel. I'd have a word or two in this matter. What is the great hurry now? Why do I have to pick up the money Sunday, rather than Monday, as previously arranged? So I went and we had a conversation.

Later we went for a car ride to look at the flood. It is a really depressing sight. The river is rising enormously but the worst is still to come according to the news on the radio. The crest will arrive when the great rush of the two rivers, the Red and the Assiniboine, will meet at Winnipeg. Many stores on Main Street are flooded and other places are full of water. They cannot be approached except by boat. A man died in a basement. He was a volunteer. They are always asking for volunteers. He was in the basement when the water suddenly rushed in and he drowned. Everyone needs to be inoculated against typhoid fever. There is one case already. No school tomorrow. "The worst is still to come." Everyone is panic-stricken and the excitement is growing. Thank God we are living higher up. Esther's mother phoned and telegraphed from California for news. Esther's friend's mother phoned from Toronto that she should immediately make arrangements to fly to Toronto.

The other day Miss Mindess told Esther that Lusia is very hard to get along with. That's why she is moving so much and no one is satisfied with her. She is not like me, said Esther. In my eyes, Miss Mindess is not a good social worker. Maybe she is nice in life but she is certainly mean in the office. Not to me, because I didn't ask her for advice or anything, but even if she doesn't like Lusia, I don't think she treated her nicely. She blamed her when she was failing and discouraged her from going into nursing. She said she shouldn't expect anything from the Congress. Of course, I know that she is not there to give but to save as much as possible.

I got a letter from Ibi [Bein] yesterday. She is in Montreal already. She is having a wonderful time and she changed her name to Aniko [Anna]. She related a story about a chicken that she bought but didn't know how to cook. Then some boys came over and each wanted to eat something different. So each one grabbed a piece of the chicken and made whatever he wanted. They let her taste it. She promised never to buy a chicken again.

May 9

There was no school today because of the flood. I got up a little after 8:00. I had to iron. I didn't expect any mail from home yet, but still, I hoped. After each piece I ironed I said to myself, "You can check for the mail after you finish this one." Meanwhile I was listening to the radio. Every few minutes there was emergency news about the flood. I don't know how many thousands of houses had to evacuate. About 14,000 people had to leave their homes.[34]

---

34 The Red River Flood lasted from April 15 to June 2, 1950. Most figures state that by the end of the flooding, 100,000 people had been evacuated from their homes.

At last, I went out to check. There was mail from Malvin. At first I didn't even know what to do, I was so happy. She is warning me of difficulties but she writes how happy everybody is that I am going home. I had tears of joy, I was so happy.

Then I went to the store. I didn't have enough money [for the streetcar] *and I had only student tickets, which I can use only at certain times, or they are for children under twelve. So I rubbed all my lipstick off my mouth and went as if under twelve. I got on the streetcar first and slipped in fast. The conductor stared at me and I pretended not to notice anything and I was in. Every house in town is flooded. The water is being piped out of basements. Now it is raining again. The house is cold because the fire is disconnected. I have a terrible headache to which Raymie* [Raymond] *and Vicky just add because they don't want to go to sleep. They yell and fight and fool around. Kathy and Lusia phoned. I don't know what is going to happen about school, but it will be too bad for me if I have to be in the store and do some things at home and won't have time to study. I better hope for school to start. At least there I am learning something. Now I have to write a letter to Rákosi* [Hungary's leader at the time] *about my going home. Then I have to take a bath because Kathy said that we may not have any hot water.*

May 10

Yesterday I was in the store the whole day. At night Lusia came over to visit. Kathy also came over to take her things. Benny phoned to say he wanted to come over but when he heard others were here, he said he'd try to bring some of his friends. But it got too late and they didn't want to come. So he phoned again saying that he'll come the next day because he wants to be with me. Darn him if he thinks he is so smart.

Then Esther came home and said she doesn't want to stay here. She was very nervous and the bad news on the radio made me very nervous, too.

Today we took the carpets and some other things upstairs. I wrote my letter to Rákosi and mailed it. I bought some stamps from the money from my examination because I haven't a cent of my own. In the after-noon I was sunbathing. Gabriel came over and we were arguing about going home [to Hungary]. *Then we went for a bike ride to see the city. I should say it looks pretty bad. The water is rising very swiftly. Later on, I went to see Olga. She says I should go to Montreal. I might like it there. I only want to be in a nicer city for a while in Canada. But it seems impossible because of Esther and the expenses. Then Olga came over and told Esther her idea. Esther said she is right, I should go. I should tell Congress that they* [the Lipkins] *are going to California and now that women and children are advised to leave the city, they should send me to Montreal. I am very nervous and I don't know what to do with myself.*

Everybody was so excited about it [the flood]; *it seemed to change so many things. Esther left for Regina with Raymond and Vicky. I felt so terrible and so lonely I could hardly bear it. I went to my room and could not help saying almost aloud, "I want to be home, I want to be home." I didn't want to go with them. I even said that to Kathy just the day before. But I realize now, again, how I don't belong to anyone. I guess I just have to learn to take things as they are.*

Miss Mindess brought me to a place [the Blumes] *where they took me in as a flood refugee. I guess it wasn't enough for me to be one once* [a refugee]. *The lady likes to talk a lot, but she means well. I don't have any obligation to them. This is important to me. There is no school at the moment and I went to work at the store.*

I wrote Ottawa [to the government] *to ask for information about going home. I was quite determined. I visited with Olga several times and I told her the situation. She said I was 100 per cent right. I even had some pictures taken that are necessary for the passport.*

It was really funny, but maybe because I have a little suntan, which suits me, people seem to be looking at me. I was running here and there every night; I couldn't make enough use of my freedom. I was having a good time. I spent some time with a certain boy who liked me. Then this got a little tiresome after a while.

Sunday I went to Olga's. Gabriel and George were there. They asked me if I wanted to go with them to Nemeth's. I said okay but I wanted to change first. I needed to go to the Lipkins and I found Esther home already. Gabriel asked, "Is Susan coming back?" Esther said it was up to me. I said nothing. I feel that she doesn't want me back and no part of me wanted to go back. How could I ever babysit again?

Gabriel and George asked if I wanted to go with them to Kildonan Park. While they were playing ball I was sunning myself. Suddenly I beheld a boy coming toward me, with whom I danced once at the Y. He [Sid] inquired whether I had anything to do tonight. Actually I planned to go to Nemeth's, but I told him I had no plans. Sid and I went for a bike ride to the park. On Monday we went out again. Tuesday he called but I wasn't at home. On Wednesday we went to a movie, and then we went out to eat. On Thursday he called on me, but I had to have a little argument with Mrs. Blumes because she didn't want me to go out. She even told Sid this, but she relented and let me go out for an hour. At the door as he was leaving Sid said, "My feeling is that you are always laughing behind my back." Maybe at first this was true because I didn't want to get burned. But then I started to believe that he really liked me and it meant a lot to me to feel that I belonged to someone and have it last for a little while. So I don't even know what got into me, I even surprised myself, because for an answer I kissed him. "I can take this for an answer," he said. Then he said, "Let's skip tomorrow, to please Mrs. Blumes, and I'll see you on Saturday." But Mrs. Blumes said she didn't mind if I went out. I went out with Kathy and Feri [Frank] to the movies. On the way we met Elek, and he came with us and paid for my ticket. I was disgusted to death with him, but just to get rid of him I promised I would go to Nemeth's. I had an awful time. I was twice as angry when I came home and found out that Sid was here. I was angry with him for not telling me he would come.

A few days ago a neighbour boy asked me if I would go to the beach with him. When I told this to Sid, he said, "You will go to the beach with me." So I told that boy that I had to work on Saturday and I could not go with him. It actually came true, as I did have to go to the store. I was paid two dollars. Darn them.

After 6:00 I went to the Lipkins for some things and I told her what had been bothering me all day — that I won't be coming back and I hope she understands. She said she did and it was all right, especially as they are leaving for California in about two months. She was even crying a little bit, too. What an actress. It seems everything has solved itself. How much of a headache all this gave me and how simply it got solved.

I often felt that somehow she put me down, not so much with what she said but how she said it. But it is okay now. They gave me a bra and a slip for my birthday. I spent much more for theirs. But that is okay, too. At least, and at last, I am rid of them. They asked me to go with them to the Nanking [restaurant] for dinner, but I thanked them and said that I had to go home as I was expecting a call.

I went home, took a bath, got dressed and was waiting for a telephone call that did not come. I didn't want to go out and was getting terribly anxious. I hate to wait for anybody. Then, at last the phone rang. It was a little girl, wanting to speak to "Sonia." Wrong number, darn it. This telephone call was very suspicious to me. Then the doorbell rang and it was Sid. We went out and when we came home he said he'd call. I told him I didn't want to sit at home all day waiting for his phone call. Which I did do, and how. Not all day, of course.

The next day I saw Ellen and spent some time with Lusia. I returned home at about 8:00 p.m. The telephone rang and someone wanted to speak to Susan. "Speaking." "What are you doing?" "Not much; reading." "Do you want to go for a walk?" "Okay; there is not much else to do today." "I'll be over in ten minutes." I was happy as I got ready to go. I ran down when the doorbell rang and opened the door. A boy was standing there and he said, "So shall we go for a walk?" I looked at him and said, "I am sure I have never seen you before." "Yes, I met you at the Y about two months ago." "I don't remember. I must have met a lot of people. Well, if you are here already, let's go for a walk." "What if the other one calls?" asked Mrs. Blumes. "I'll be back soon." As we were *walking, I felt like embarrassing him. "This is very funny but I am sure I never met you before." "But I did." "Why didn't you say what your name was when you called? Even if I met you I wouldn't know who you were on the phone." He was apologetic. I persevered by asking, "How did you get my telephone number?" "You gave it to me." "Impossible; I didn't live here two months ago. Who gave you my number?" He said, "Gabi." So I told him that I was very sorry, I was expecting someone else's call and that now I had to go home because I had a date. He then proceeded to tell me a story with a very poor imagination. Poor story. But in spite of my disappointment, I had to laugh. "Can I see you on Saturday?" "I don't know yet. You can phone me up sometime. Goodbye." But I was still supposed to go for a walk with Hillel, the neighbour boy. I was close to bursting already. So Mrs. Blumes and I were to go for a walk, as I didn't have patience to sit at home. But dear Hillel was sitting on the porch. Mrs. Blumes was ignoring my gesticulations and changed her mind about going for a walk and sent us to [go for a walk]. I came home soon.*

When I am not at home, everyone is trying to get me: Gabriel, Elek, Hillel, even Sid. But when I am waiting for a call, it just keeps quiet. Darn.

Monday

Kathy called me early in the morning to tell me she broke up with Frank. She really deserves respect for deciding to do it. She says he takes out Rozsi, a little Hungarian girl. I don't know what you would call her in English. This really hurts her. I hope she gets over it soon. She'll have many other boyfriends. This reminds me, Anton asked her once if I would stay in Canada if he offered to marry me. Ha. Not bad eh? "You don't think that Susan wants you," she said. This is good for a laugh. Poor boy wants desperately to get married.

He [Sid] didn't phone today either. I feel just horrible. I will get over it; I will feel better; I'll get it out of my system. I am not in love with him; this is only another disappointment, a little kick in the heart. I didn't want to take it to heart, but somehow he made me believe that he liked me. I wanted to hang on to even a little bit of him liking me. I didn't like anybody for such a long time and I had to get a crush just when I started feeling human.

Sid called and we went to the circus. We went to visit Kathy. On Sunday we were together and he was fixing my bike. Afterwards, Sid, Lusia and I went for a bike ride. On Monday I went to the movies with Gabi. Sid phoned though I told him I wouldn't be at home. On Tuesday, we met by accident, and later he came over. Later on, I visited Ellen. She is having a baby. On Wednesday, we met at Kathy's. On Thursday I was babysitting from 8:30 till 11:45. I was paid one dollar.

I had a party. It was classy. Sid gave me a camera for my birthday [June 3]. He was so sweet.

Kathy had to go to a T.B. hospital. I went with her today.

I have my exams next week and I've pretty much not done any studying.

Part Two: Memoir

Author's Preface

Whenever I meet someone from Hungary, I feel an immediate empathy and love I haven't felt for such a long time, as well as a sense of gratitude for having the privilege to experience such a strong feeling. A great part of this emotion, I believe, is a shared past.

I have resided in Canada for over seventy years, but whenever I refer to Budapest, I call it home. In trying to explain this to myself, and to understand my underlying feelings, I found a German word, of all things, that seems to fit my strong and deep attachment to the sense of my first home. The word is *Heimat*, and it is hard to define in English. In an interview with Eleanor Wachtel on the C B C radio show Writers & Company, author Nora Krug described the word *Heimat* — which is also the title of her new book — by saying, "To me, the word is closely related to my childhood. It represents an almost utopian state of mind, something that is gone and that I can't recapture but that I hold onto in some way. I have deeply emotional connotations with it…." She captured almost exactly my sense of the word, which sometimes translates to "belonging."

I believe my memoir is about two concepts, love and home, which are most important in a human being's life. Going back to the far recesses of my mind, I remember that I first wrote about the loss of these two things, this something irreplaceable, in my diary of long ago. At such an early age, I was deprived of love, security and comfort

— little by little, year by year. First by my father — saying goodbye to him at age nine is seared into my brain. Then my mother, when she left me alone at a time of extreme danger. Recalling my goodbye with my father, I knew then that there was a possibility of my mother being gone from me forever. As a child, I realized the precariousness of my own life.

Then, just a few years later, I left an extremely loving and doting family in Hungary for a strange land, Canada, where I immediately encountered what I felt was the highest degree of culture shock and powerlessness as an immigrant. I believe that being an immigrant changed how I was seen and how I saw myself. I lived a life of overwhelming loneliness, where I felt that nobody loved and cared for me. But I eventually overcame this and created a life for myself and for my family. My children had the opportunity in life to do what they wished. So do my grandchildren. I did what I could. This is my life, and I have to be satisfied with it.

Capturing Images

My relatives described the momentous occasion of my birth to me. They told me that when my father went to see his mother to inform her of my birth, his face was white and he said, "Mama, it's a girl." I took this to mean that he was disappointed at not having a son. In spite of that, I thought this story laughable because I knew how much he adored me, and I was positive that there was no way he would have traded me for a son.

I was born at the Alice Weiss Maternity Hospital on June 3, 1933, the same year that Hitler came to power in Germany, to Magdolna (Magda, or Magdus) and Bernat Löffler. I was named Zsuzsanna Veronika, and my Hebrew name is Eszter. I was a skinny little kid. I did not like to eat, and I remember thinking that mealtimes were the worst part of my day. While my mother would try to feed me, my father would tell me stories to distract me. Once, my mother was feeding me spinach while I was listening to a story; after a while I blew the spinach out of my mouth and all over the kitchen walls.

My parents married on September 2, 1932. They were both very beautiful. My mother had a picture taken by a photographer when she was eighteen years old, and it was displayed in the window of the photographer's studio. My cousin Bandi, who was a young boy at the time, told me that he used to take his friends to see it and boast about his aunt's good looks.

My mother was quiet and reserved, while my father was outgoing and very sociable. An extrovert, he liked people and he liked to talk; he would corner anybody and talk their ears off. As a young man he was an amateur actor and he wrote poetry, which I memorized and recited at plays my friends and I put on. My father liked to go to the movies and would buy the tickets ahead of time. Although sometimes my mother didn't want to go, I loved going to movies. I remember being so excited when the Hollywood MGM lion appeared and roared, turning its head. I could hardly wait for the movie to begin. (I remember, though, that the wicked witch in *The Wizard of Oz* gave me nightmares. And another children's movie, *The Blue Bird*, with Shirley Temple, sent me jumping out of my seat and out into the foyer, my aunt running after me. I was frightened to death by the scene of the fire in the forest.)

My father had a typewriter business called Hungaria Irogep Vallalat (Hungarian Typewriter Company), which he ran out of our apartment. He sold typewriters and also rented them and fixed them. He would have liked to be a doctor, but the *numerus clausus,* a law restricting the number of Jews who could attend higher education, prevented that dream. My father had to work to help support his parents, and I had a sense that my father's family wasn't happy when he got married. There was not a warm relationship between my mother and his family.

My father had a delivery man, whom I called Uncle Landler, and two typists — small Lilli and big Lilli — if someone required typing of handwritten papers or documents. My mother also worked at home. She repaired carpets, very valuable ones such as Persian and Smyrna, which needed an artist's touch.

When I was three years old, we moved into an apartment on Péterfy Sándor utca 17, III 24, across from the Mabi hospital in the 7th district of Budapest. I knew all the neighbours in our apartment building — I particularly remember the Abonyis, the Horvaths, the Löwys, the Weiszs and the Wilheims. We had a two-bedroom apartment with a bathroom and a kitchen, which included a maid's room. We weren't rich, but we were comfortable, and I don't remember missing anything I needed in my young life. I was an only child, and one thing I did greatly desire was a sibling. I even imagined somehow acquiring a baby, hiding it and looking after it.

In our home, there was no automatic heating. In the corner of one room, there was a ceramic stove where one could make a fire with either coal or wood. It had to be started early in the morning to warm up the room. Before my mother woke me up each morning, she would gently pull my feet out from under the covers and put socks on my feet. My mother would also rub my socks to make them softer. No clothes dryer existed, at least not for us.

As an only child, I believe my parents adored me. I loved them both, but I especially adored my father. He always encouraged me to be independent and self-reliant, traits that helped me later on. I loved when my father told me stories about when he was a little boy. One was about when he started school and had long blond curly hair. He was told that if his hair wasn't cut, he would have to attend the girls' class. He used to tell me made-up stories too, about characters named Iniwini Minnie and Incifinci Manci. He would amuse me with these stories, especially when I was sick. He helped me learn to read and do the multiplication table. I loved my father very much.

Once, there was a silly question going around that children were asking each other — who do you love more, your father or your mother? Of course, the answer should be both the same. But I remember, in a moment of adoration, whispering to my father, "I love you the most." He seemed pleased but made me promise that this was to be our secret, never to be mentioned to my mother.

Even so, my mother was beautiful and wonderful, albeit more reserved than my father. She was hardworking and artistic, and cleanliness was very important to her. Whenever I was away from home, I longed to be with her — more than longed, actually. I insisted with such force and stubbornness that I always made it happen. Those were times when I was supposed to enjoy a holiday away from the heat of the big city. But I just wanted to be with her.

My father was the middle child in his family, born in 1904. He had an older sister, Berta, who never married, and a younger sister Bözsi (Erzsebet, or Elizabeth in English), who married Jozef Herman. I have no doubt that my father was the favourite. As of this writing, I do not know of one single relative on my father's side. My father's father, Jozsef Löffler, was the only grandparent of mine who died while I was very young. I remember him being in a wheelchair, and my father visiting his family daily and bathing his father. I believe I was five when he died. At the unveiling of his gravestone, my father's eyes were red from crying, and that made an indelible impression on me. I have my father's *yizkor* book for his father. My father had filled in the space for all the forthcoming *yizkor* dates, up until 1964. Of course, he was unable to fulfill that duty, but clearly, he had the intention to.

My mother was born in 1910 in Szilágypér, then part of Hungary (Transylvania), and now part of Romania. Her parents were Farkas and Eszter Weisz. My grandparents were very religious. My grandmother kept kosher and observed all the holidays and Shabbat. My mother was the second youngest of her five siblings — Ilus, Malvin, Bözsi, Lajos and Ibolya (Ibi).

My oldest aunt, Ilus, was a widow. She had one son, Andor Osztermann (Bandi), who is eleven years older than me. They lived with my grandparents. Ilus was a businesswoman. From my understanding, her husband was a gambler and ended up killing himself when he lost his money.

My aunt Malvin was married to Géza Pollak and had a daughter, Ágnes, six years older than me. My aunt Bözsi was married to Sandor Nagy, a gentile. Naturally, my grandparents were totally against them getting married, even threatening to consider my aunt dead and sit shiva if they married. They had to promise to keep kosher and bring up their children Jewish. Their daughter, Éva, was four years older than me. They had a house in Zugló, on the outskirts of Budapest. My uncle had an important position at one of the newspapers. He gave me books for Christmas, which made me very happy, and he was very kind. Having a Christian uncle became very helpful during the German occupation.

Uncle Lajos was the only son, the one who would say Kaddish for his parents. He was relatively well off and had a store. There was always an expectation that he help out with supporting my grandparents. From the stories I heard from my aunts, he didn't always come through, not enough at least. He was married to Auntie Magda. They had a daughter, Marietta (Marika), four years younger than me. After the war, a son was born. My uncle was overjoyed. We went to his son's bris by taxi (nobody in my family had cars at that time). Tragically, that boy turned out to be mentally disabled. This was blamed on the hardships my aunt and uncle had endured in the war.

My youngest aunt was Ibolya (meaning "violet" in English). Ibi was pretty and vivacious. She had married and then divorced, and then remarried my uncle Pista Rona during the later part of the war.

My mother's family was very close knit and always spent time together — Shabbat dinners at my grandparents and get-togethers on Saturday evenings to play cards. Some Saturdays, my parents, Malvin, Géza, Ilus and Bandi all went to the movies together. On Sundays in the summer, the whole family would go to Csillaghegy or the Széchenyi, swimming resorts, or somewhere by boat or on excursions to the mountains of Buda. We also went to Lake Balaton as a family, or sometimes I went just with my parents.

My older cousin Bandi, who had lived with my grandparents, told me his memories of our family before he died. I was always bugging family who were older than me to tell me their memories, as they could remember more than I could. When I visited him once, Bandi remarked that it was too painful for him to talk about the past. That remark upset me greatly, the fact that he had it in his power to throw me some crumbs, which I hungered for, and did not want to make the effort. I didn't visit him for a while after that. But another time he did talk about the past, and although it was nothing that I hadn't known before, I appreciated it. He spoke about how the family was extremely close, and about going to exercise with my father. My father was very strong, and it seemed like he could do push-ups forever. His biceps bulged when he made a fist. I remember admiring them, and I called them "turtles."

Bandi said that the family was so close they did not need or have many friends outside the family. But I remember my father's friends Jeno and Kato Schtricher, and another couple, although I don't remember seeing them with my mother after my father was gone. Bandi worked as a furrier and made my father a fur vest, which my mother took to him when he was in the labour battalion.

I wasn't aware of when the war years started, but I am sure my parents were. One day when my father arrived home, he slapped me. I never got over the shock of that, because I could not understand why. Now I believe he must have been extremely stressed. Much later in life, when I listened to my aunt Magda reminisce about the past, she told me that when my father was called up and forced to join the labour battalion for Jewish men in 1942, he came to say his goodbyes to her. He said, "I am going into the fire." He literally did, and also to the frozen fields of the Soviet Union.

The first time my father was taken, he was released on account of a medical condition. He returned home at dawn, appearing at the window of our bedroom, which faced a courtyard. I climbed into bed with my parents while he related his experiences. I remember the overwhelming joy of having him home. I was at home alone when he received his next call-up. I opened the envelope, and knew what it meant. I cried bitterly. I didn't want him to leave us again. As young as I was, I sensed the dangers that lay ahead. It was the fall or winter of 1942 when we said our goodbyes to him.

Some time later, we received permission to visit him. My mother, my aunt Ilus and I went by train to some remote camp. I was eagerly waiting to see him, as I missed him so much. When we arrived at our destination, he looked haggard and sad. He asked why we didn't bring his mother. He said he might never see her again. After a while the men had to line up to return to their base. I walked alongside my father for as long as I could. I will never forget his face — eyes red with unshed tears, with an expression of such sadness and an intense look that I felt was meant to capture and hold my image in his mind. It is with that expression on his face that I remember my father most clearly. We never heard from him again.

Eventually, my father's unit was sent to the front, to the Soviet Union or Ukraine, where the greatest fighting was happening. The Axis powers were losing and started withdrawing from the Red Army's power. Circumstances were horrible for all, but worse for the helpless Jewish men who were hated by the withdrawing armies and used cruelly.

We received notification from the International Red Cross that my father disappeared on the Eastern Front in the spring of 1943. I was nine years old. Sometime after the war, we tried to find out exactly what had happened to him. My aunt Malvin and I went to visit a woman whose husband was in the same labour battalion as my father, but she had no information for us. At one point, I heard that his group might have been in or near a hospital in Korocha, Russia, that was burnt down, from where people were shot trying to escape, but I do not know if that is true.

So then it was just the two of us, my mother and I. She continued on with my father's business, hiring a repairman to substitute for him. After my father was gone, I visited my paternal grandmother, Roza, regularly. My mother took me there but didn't come in herself. Later on, I visited her and my aunts regularly on my own. I was the only grandchild, and I am sure they adored me. My mother and I continued on with our lives as normally as possible under the circumstances. At times I was able to be of some help in the family business. By doing so, I was very proud of myself and felt very important.

My life centred on going to school and playing with friends. We children amused ourselves by playing house a lot, and hide-and-seek. We always had to blindfold a seeker because the places to hide were pretty limited. I considered those games lots of fun. I think I was a strong-willed child, probably pretty spoiled and sometimes disobedient. I had a temper and stamped my feet when I didn't get my way. But I had lots of friends and I loved to visit them. Our neighbourhood was safe, and I was allowed to come and go by myself. In Grade 1 my friends were Vera (Csoppi) Schwartz, Magda Steiner, Marika Székely, Ági Brecher, Jutka Haar, Vera Roth and Zsuzsi Lausch, who was my best friend. After the war, all of these girls settled in various places — the United States, Austria, Canada, Israel and Australia. I kept in touch with some of them.

Jutka Haar and I became good friends very quickly. When she had first appeared at the door of our class in mid-season and the teacher sat her next to me, I didn't want to sit next to her because I thought she wasn't pretty. But we soon visited each other all the time. She lived with her aunt, uncle and cousin, Otto Krausz. They were poor, living in a one-room apartment. Her parents were among the first Jews to be taken away and killed, the first to have that fate. In 1941, Jews of Polish origin who did not have Hungarian citizenship were murdered at Kamenets-Podolsk. So Jutka was not only the first orphan I knew, but, most importantly, hearing her story was the first realization I had that the Germans were killing Jews.

One summer, my mother arranged for me to go to Lake Balaton to enjoy a vacation away from the big city. My mother found a family who would take me with them if she paid them for my keep. The people I stayed with warned me not to mention that I was Jewish. Later on, my young cousin Marietta, who was a very pretty little girl, came to stay with us. I overheard someone remark, "What a shame she is Jewish." As if good looks were wasted on a Jewish child. Yet what a prophetic remark that was.

The next summer, I went to stay with my cousin Ági's grandparents at Paks, a small town by the Danube River. They had a foster daughter, Ilonka, who was around my age. I was very homesick (one of many times) and I wrote a letter to my mother with many complaints in it (possibly some of them made up in desperation). One morning when I woke up I thought my mother was lying next to me, having come to take me home. I was very disappointed to find that it was only my cousin Ági there. The following summer, Ági's grandparents and Ilonka were taken to Auschwitz. I felt terrible for not keeping up the correspondence with Ilonka, as I had promised her. Tears fill my eyes as I write about this. It is all too horrible for words.

Waiting in Vain

On June 3, 1943, my tenth birthday, I received a thank-you note from the O M Z S A, the Jewish Aid Association, for a good deed — my friend Marika Aschenfeld and I had raised money for the agency by putting on a play and also by selling a few of our things. I still have that note.

Later that year, I went into public school, but I hoped to eventually transfer to the Jewish *gimnázium* for higher education. At that time, an occasional air raid was the only reminder to us that a war was going on. Just before a geography test, we kids even prayed for one. However, in March 1944, our school was closed. When the Germans marched in and occupied Hungary, all plans for the future became uncertain.

My friends and I were planning to put on another play to raise money for the Jewish Aid Association. The performance was scheduled for Sunday afternoon, March 19, 1944. We were all very excited about it, and we had had our final rehearsal in the morning. As my friend Ági and I were leaving for home, we met up with her older sister, Lily, who seemed extremely agitated and urged us to hurry home as fast as we could. She made us take the streetcar, a short distance we would usually walk. When we got off the streetcar, Lily whispered, "The Germans are here." My thoughts were racing with a frightening knowledge, originating I knew not from where — the Germans are killing Jews. My eyes started tearing and I found myself running home.

When I related my news at home, no one wanted to believe me. But soon enough, the bad news was confirmed. My cousins Gabi and Olga, who were staying with us, were frantic with one desire: to go home to Nagyvárad and be with their family. By then we heard that travel was unsafe; Jews were being arrested and taken off trains, and we did not know where they were taken to. Soon after that I started writing a diary, in which I described the events as I was aware of them.

By the beginning of April 1944, we were ordered to wear the yellow star. Early in the morning, at the first opportunity, my mother went out wearing it to prove that she wasn't ashamed of it. She was brave and proud to be Jewish, not ashamed and cowering, as many other people were. One time, I fought with somebody who called me a name. I wasn't taking it lying down.

By June 1944, our building had turned into a yellow-star house, a designated Jewish house in Budapest. People moved into our apartment, including my mother's cousin Mimi Koves and her son, Peter (whom I still keep in touch with). I knew we needed money and I tried to think of things to do to make some. Suzie Löwy got a job for us sewing clothes for tiny dolls; I have no idea how much we were paid, and I don't know how I even did this because I really couldn't sew. But I guess the expectation wasn't too high. I also offered to babysit my cousin Marietta and hoped to get a little pay in return. I picked her up and took her to the park and stuff like that, but of course I never asked for money, and I never got any. I also offered to help my aunt Ibi with her sewing. She was a dressmaker. I would walk to her place on Andrássy út and she would give me things to do, but alas, no money in return.

During those times, the young people who lived in our apartment building — Évi Fohn, Pali and Pötyi Wilheim, Suzie and I — put on a play. I remember a song we sang, an old slavery song that we changed the words to. In Hungarian, we sang: "Sadness pursues me; my heart is breaking; my ancient land is calling to me, where our people were happy, weren't beggars and slaves. The river is glowing; the moon is

Rumours were rampant about the goings-on outside, about groups of people marching on the street — we heard that the Jewish houses on either side of us were emptied and that the Jews were being led to God knows where. I was frantic with fear and terrified for my life. There was nowhere to go. I was convinced that whoever was removed would be killed. What else could they do with us with the Russians almost on our doorstep? The gate to our building was locked and we couldn't leave. I begged my mother to get a message to my gentile uncle to try to get us some false papers, to get us out somehow. I could not imagine dying. She agreed to ask a gentile neighbour to do it. My uncle himself came for us, but the superintendent refused to let us leave. I remember trying to figure out some escape route, but of course there was none.

We feared for the worst. A few weeks later the Arrow Cross men came with gendarmes and policemen. They entered our building and ordered us all to come down to the courtyard, where they sorted us according to age. My mother was among the women who were instructed to immediately pack and be ready to leave. One man timidly inquired whether he may remain, as his fiftieth birthday was imminent. He was allowed to stay.

The expression on my mother's face as we said goodbye was familiar. I remembered it as the same one my father wore when I last saw him — an intensive stare meant to capture and hold my image. At that time, as young as I was, I'd sensed that I wouldn't see him again. I was glad that, at least, my mother had some money with her — it was the money I had earned from my sewing, months earlier.

The next day, my friend Susie's relative Ibi, who had been taken along with my mother, managed to escape from the Arrow Cross and returned home. She told me that she asked my mother to come with her, but my mother was afraid and didn't dare. Someone else had tried and was caught and shot in front of them. This woman had begged to be spared, saying she had a small son at home, but to no avail. My shining; I will be happy again to be Hebrew and may the Jordan Rive: carry our song along."

We thought that we were brave.

As I mentioned, what I did know at the time, I recorded in m₁ diary. On October 10 I wrote, "We are living through very importan₁ times." Rumours were that the Hungarian government had asked the Soviets for a truce and got it but were afraid to make it public, fearing German retribution. How wonderful if true, I thought.

But when, on October 15, 1944, Horthy announced his intention to extricate Hungary from the war, the fate of the Budapest Jews took a turn for the worse. I was totally aware at the time what the date of October 15, 1944, meant. I wrote about it clearly in my diary. I had already heard the rumours that Horthy wanted to pull out of the war, which the Axis powers was clearly losing, and then I heard about Horthy's speech on the radio. The Soviet army entered Hungary in September and was on the outskirts of Budapest.

I was walking home from my aunt Malvin's when I met Pötyi in front of our building; I stopped to chat with her, and then her cous-in Évi came running out of the building and, breathless, told us the good news that Horthy had made a speech announcing Hungary's surrender to the Allies. That meant the end of the German rule over Hungary. We were free! I was happy beyond belief. I was saved; my life wasn't in danger anymore. It was a momentous occasion, moving from fear of death to liberation. Everybody was overjoyed.

This happiness didn't last long. The next morning was a grey, foggy day. I woke up to the sound of gunfire, and fear returned to my heart. I wondered what was going on. My mother tried to set my mind at ease, telling me not to worry, but she failed to reassure me. My fears were well-founded, we soon found out. Hungary wasn't surrendering. The Germans kidnapped Horthy's son, forcing Horthy to resign, and the fascist Arrow Cross Party, also called the Nyilas, took possession of the government, with Ferenc Szálasi, a ruthless Jew-hater, as its leader. The Nyilas were thugs, robbers and criminals.

mother must have thought that, at thirty-four, she was young and strong and would survive.

After I was left alone, I wondered what to do. We had just received some conversion papers in the hope that they might help us. I wanted to find a way to take them to my mother, but I did not know where she was. My aunt Malvin had come to take me to stay with her, and she soon took me to a nunnery. I stood in front of a big wooden gate, waiting for it to be opened, with my heart in my throat. My aunt asked if they would take me in. I was a small, very blond, blue-eyed, small-nosed child, not at all a stereotypical Jewish child. Also, with the Soviet army already at the outskirts of Budapest, the amount of time I needed to be hidden would have been very short; yet, the answer was a (regretful) no.

Next, my aunt Malvin and I stood in line with hundreds of people to get papers to get into a protected Red Cross building on Columbus Street. Hours later my aunt told me to go wait for her at home. I saw groups of people on the road with packages, being led I knew not where. I suspected the worst. My fear was overwhelming. What if the people were taken from the house to which I was returning? Where would I go? What would I do?

We did end up at the Columbus Street building, but not for long. I was with my aunt Malvin, her daughter, Ági, and Ági's boyfriend's mother and sister. The Nyilas came for us, and soon we were being marched down the road. We heard that someone who had tried to escape was shot. At one place we were stopped to be sorted, women and men of a certain age from children. My aunt wouldn't allow either me or Ági to leave her. Then we were marched to the ghetto.

When I saw the wall of the ghetto it was a horrible sensation — I believed this to be the end. I heard rumours that the Nazis' plan was to blow up the ghetto. It was the beginning of December and the ghetto was not yet sealed off. I decided to leave. I just walked out, and the guard at the gate did not stop me. I walked to Zugló, to the house of my aunt Bözsi, who was married to my gentile uncle. They couldn't keep me, as they themselves weren't safe. My aunt took me to a Red Cross children's home, where there were many children who were much younger than me. There was no hot water and no food. I bathed the children in cold water; many had scurvy and lice.

I remember a visitor, a young man wearing a Nyilas armband. I knew he was Jewish. My aunt Bözsi also came to visit me, or maybe she only came to show me a postcard from my mother, which my mother had written from the forced march to Austria. My mother must have known to send it to her address because Bözsi was married to my non-Jewish uncle, Sandor, and they were still living in their home. My mother sent several postcards from the death march they were taken on toward Austria. Many died along the way. I wasn't aware of any of the other postcards until my aunt Malvin's death in 1967.[35] She kept them in an envelope, on which was written, "Our darling Magdus's last messages." I was told that she thought it would be too devastating and heartbreaking for me to read them. Maybe she herself didn't want to part with them.

At dawn one day the Nyilas came to the children's home, and we were supposed to leave with them. I escaped through a basement window and went to my aunt's again. This time, my uncle took me to stay with his sister who was living outside of Budapest. Her son, a soldier who had deserted, was hiding there too. I had lice but I was embarrassed to tell her. I felt terrible about it, especially because we were sleeping in the same bed. I think the whole place just contained one bed. But I remember that the location was beautiful — a deserted area where I could go outside and look out into the distance.

I was terribly miserable and lonesome, to the point that I begged, insisted, that they let me return to Budapest. (I know that throughout my life, this is a recurring theme, that I am unhappy and want

---

35 The postcards and translations are on pages 162–171.

to go back home.) They let me. The train I took on Christmas Day back to Budapest was the very last one for a long time. By afternoon, the Soviets had occupied the town I had been in. When I arrived at Budapest's railway station, I found that no streetcars were running in the city. So I started walking to Zugló, to my aunt's house.

Because of the Soviet army moving westward, there were many refugees — non-Jewish Hungarians — fleeing east, away from them. In the chaos and the turmoil of the times it was easy to blend in and claim refugee status. And I was equipped with false papers.[36] I just had to memorize the details of who I was.

As I was walking toward Zugló, a young boy who was going in the same direction joined me. Our conversation naturally turned to who we were, what we were doing, where we were going. I was scared to death about giving myself away, and not just myself but my aunt and cousin who lived in the house in Zugló and who counted as Jewish just as any other Jew did, though so far nobody had come for them.

When I arrived at the house, I couldn't hide my fears and worries from them, and I told them about the boy I had been speaking with. My uncle threatened to leave. Maybe he did; now I am not sure. But I remember understanding his situation and feeling bad for him, and also feeling bad that I was the cause. (I may have told the boy, unthinkingly, where I was setting out to.) I wet the bed there, and the next morning Éva lifted up the sheet in front of the window to show everyone. I was horribly embarrassed and never forgot it, but this incident was never mentioned later on.

Because of the danger in me being with them, my aunt Bözsi took me to stay with Aunt Ilus, who was also hiding with false papers. My beloved aunt Ilus, who was hiding in an apartment with a gentile friend of hers, was paying her for having us there.

I had arrived back in Budapest just as the siege was beginning,

---

36 Susan does not recall how she got the false identity document, but thinks that it was likely from her uncle.

and it lasted for fifty days, until the whole of Budapest was liberated on February 13.

The entire city of Budapest was surrounded by the Soviets. Now the German and Hungarian armies were fighting the Soviet army from street to street and house to house, bombs were falling and there was shooting and shelling. Now I was to endure the siege of the city as well as the danger and fear of being caught by the Arrow Cross.

Because my aunt Ilus looked Jewish, I was the one who went out to look for food when the lentils my aunt had brought with her ran out. During the siege there was hardly any food in Budapest for anybody, regardless of whether they were Jewish or not. We got ration coupons to get about two slices of black bread, and I would go out early in the morning to stand in line in front of a bakery. What stands out in my mind is the time when a shell hit right above our heads. Dust surrounded everything, and I couldn't find my way out of it. It was a very traumatic experience.

The next time I went out, I was so hungry that I felt that it didn't matter whether I died of hunger or from being hit by a shell. I decided to go to my aunt Bözsi's house to get some food. As I walked, I saw dead horses on the street and people cutting the horsemeat for food. Not a usual sight. I also saw dead bodies lying on the streets. As I passed the ghetto, I saw a pile of bodies, one thrown on top of another to form a hill. Planes were flying and dropping bombs, guns were firing and there was constant shelling. The noise was increasing to the point that I was too scared to continue walking. I stopped to consider what to do. As I wrote in my diary, I saw a man wearing an Arrow Cross armband. I figured that if I approached him, he would not think I was Jewish. So I did. I asked him if it was possible to go to Zugló. He replied, "Little girl, you better go home. The Russians have taken Zugló."

I was about fifteen minutes away from the front line! Just then I was passing my aunt Malvin's apartment house, where I knew a gentile friend of hers lived. These people, the Kis family, fed me until I was full and kept me overnight. They also told me where my aunt Ibi and her husband, Pista, were hiding. I proceeded to go there. I found them living in a basement, as at this point in time, everyone was living underground on account of the siege. They were living with the Feher family, who had a little daughter named Iren. As we played "school" together, I had to be extremely cautious about what I told her I had learned in school, specifically around religion. She gave me a picture of herself as a memento when we parted.

The shooting and the bombing and the firing kept on, unabated. And then one day, silence. I went up from the basement and looked around outside. On the corner of the street I beheld a Soviet soldier, our liberator. We were free. The realization that I was alive, that I had survived, seemed miraculous.

Then the waiting began. People started arriving back from the concentration camps. We waited and waited. Everybody waited for someone. And those who survived returned. And the families of those who did not make it waited in vain.

When I was liberated, I immediately went to my aunt Bözsi's house. Living on the outskirts of Budapest, their area had been the first part of the city to be liberated. All through the Nazi occupation, my aunt Bözsi and my cousin Éva had remained in their house; although they were Jewish, and were certainly considered 100 per cent Jewish by the authorities, they were not denounced by their neighbours or by anyone else. In that sense, they were lucky. When I arrived there, my cousin Éva had a big hole in her cheek. She had been sitting by a window that shattered and fell on her.

Very soon after our liberation, I was walking with my friend Ági Schonberger on Andrássy út, near a place where Soviet soldiers were stationed. As a soldier was walking by us, Ági told me to ask him for bread, and I did. He nodded to me to follow him into the house. I did so reluctantly, as we were cognizant of rumours about Soviet soldiers raping women. He took me into an empty room and told me to wait. He returned with a loaf of bread. I thanked him and he kissed me on the cheek. Ági and I shared the bread. I took my share to my maternal grandmother, Eszter.

112 TOO MANY GOODBYES

Later, I went to visit my friend Jutka Haar; she told me that she and her cousin were going to Debrecen with the Zionist group Hanoar Hatzioni and I decided I wanted to go, too. We went on a train that was so full we hardly had room to stand. People were hanging off the steps and were also on the roof. The train was so crowded that when I lifted one foot up, I found no space to put it back down. Everybody was travelling east for food.

The people in charge of our group brought us to a bombed-out villa, which had to be fixed and cleaned out before we could move in. We were a group of children with several younger adults who were the counsellors in charge of us. Some of us were placed with a family, while for others, space was provided in the villa. Judit and I were placed with a man and his son, who would also provide us with breakfast. I vividly recall the son saying that he had a girlfriend and that if she returned, he would walk through the whole city on his knees. Jutka and I had another place to go for our supper — the Mullers'. We would also go and have a meal with the rest of the gang. So I believe we (or I) averaged two meals for each one. The Mullers seemed to be quite wealthy. They had a big house, and the table was always set for a full dinner. The younger daughter's name was Judit, and she was about our age. Her older sister had a boyfriend. When our clothes were disinfected (deloused) and I had left my money in them, I was upset, and the boyfriend replaced my money.

Eventually we all moved into the villa. It was pleasant being together with the children, but I did not hear anything about my parents. One girl's mother did return and came to get her. We were divided into groups called *kvutzot* in Hebrew and kept busy with some activities. Once, we were supposed to write an essay about Palestine. One counsellor named Arjey took me aside and questioned whether I had really written mine by myself. We also put on plays. I recited a poem by a renowned Hebrew poet, Hayim Nahman Bialik, and the kids teased me afterwards because instead of speaking it, I sang the lines, "Dalolj, dalolj kis madarkam, a földről ahol a tavasz örök." (Sing, sing

little bird, about the land where spring is eternal.) One boy and I
started liking each other and sometimes we walked together hand in
hand. His name was Otto Weisz, and he later wrote me a letter from
Cyprus. I answered him but never heard from him again. Jutka Haar's
cousin Otto Krausz also liked me, but I didn't like him back. When
I used to visit Jutka a lot, Otto started to teach us chess. His father
had been taken to Auschwitz and he told me he couldn't imagine his
father being only smoke. I got attached to one of the male counsellors
who also showed me some affection. He was a nice-looking young
man. He had a bullet wound in his stomach.

We went to elementary school (which was what was available
there) very half-heartedly. I used to fall asleep in class. We probably
went to sleep very late. I remember going to the market where there
was fruit displayed, which of course we could not afford to buy. I
tasted it, pretending to see if I liked it before I bought it.

Eventually I had no clothes to wear. I don't know if I had grown
out of mine or if it was just that by then it was summer and warm. I
remember borrowing Otto's pants. Then my aunt Malvin came and
brought some material. We went to a dressmaker who made me two
summer dresses. One was red with white polka dots, the other, blue.
My running shoes were so small that I had to cut out the front of the
shoes so that my toes could extend out of them.

I think that by then I realized that my parents were not returning.
I was getting very lonely and I really wanted to go home. I wrote to
Bandi, who for some reason I believed was buying food somewhere
in the area, to come and get me.

Eventually I went home. I think I had been there about four
months. I was told later that the reason my family had left me in
Debrecen so long was that everyone was so heartbroken. The whole
family was having a terrible time, and Aunt Malvin, who had been
in the Budapest ghetto with my grandparents, was seriously ill with
pneumonia. After I returned from Debrecen, I started living with my
aunt Malvin, whose husband, Géza, had not returned from a con-

centration camp. She was extremely good to me, as good as a mother could be. I felt that all of my mothers' family loved and cared for me a lot, particularly at that time. I felt totally at ease at any time to stay anywhere my family lived and I knew they would welcome me. I felt they loved me for myself and for my mother, too. I missed my parents dreadfully, yet I carried on with my life.

~

Throughout the years, I tried very hard to find out what happened to my mother. With a lot of research and effort, and some luck, I was able to find some information on Lichtenwörth, where my mother had been held. My aunt Bözsi, my father's sister, was in the same camp as my mother. When Aunt Bözsi returned home, she was shocked to find that my mother hadn't made it back. When the camp was liberated, my aunt had been taking care of a cousin who was sick. My mother told my aunt that she was sorry she could not wait for her, but she had to leave right away to come back home to me.

After liberation, I went to see some of the women who had returned from the camp in Lichtenwörth. It turned out that my mother had gotten sick as she was walking home and had died in a makeshift hospital in an Austrian town called Neudörfl. Much later, my cousin Robi found out that my mother had died on April 20, 1945, at 2:15 in the afternoon. That is what it says in the town's death registry. Because I know the exact date of my mother's death, I can light the yahrzeit candle in her honour on the appropriate date. My mother was buried along with two other Jewish women on the outskirts of a Roman Catholic cemetery. She was thirty-four years old.

To add to my grief and sorrow about her death is the fact that she died without knowing if I, her parents, or the rest of the family were alive. And all alone, with no one who loved her. I believe with all my heart that someone who dies surrounded by loving family is lucky.

The Decision

Since I had missed a whole year of school, I started studying with one of my former teachers to write exams and make up for that year. What I remember about studying with that teacher is that often, when I glanced at her, I saw that she was making grimacing faces. I found it very uncomfortable; I believed she was in great pain (from a sickness or a physical pain) and I tried to pretend I did not notice because I did not know what else to do, being only twelve years old. Now I think perhaps it was mental pain, grieving. Who knows what people thought or felt or what they were going through at that time?

I had only a very short time to study and write exams before the school year would begin, but I did it, and in the fall I passed into my regular class. I started going back to public school in September with many of my old friends. I became an excellent student. Ági *néni*, an older friend whom I fell in love with (perhaps as a substitute for my mother?), thought I was a genius. We could talk with each other about everything, and we read poetry together. I understood mathematics before it was even explained. I could visualize it.

The only thing I wasn't great at was art, because I couldn't draw for the life of me. I hoped it wouldn't ruin my chances to transfer the following year to the Jewish *gimnázium*, which was my dream. And it did not. The next summer I again had to study to write exams to be able to transfer from public school to the *gimnázium*, as the curriculum had a much higher standard and different subject matter. At that, I again excelled, to the extent that my home teacher, Erzsi *néni,* asked me to tutor another girl to write the same exams the following year.

That summer I also went to Hashomer Hatzair camp, which was memorable. I had been attending the Zionist group meetings and had met many friends, including Gizi (Ilonka) Weisz, Zsuzsi Fabian and Anita Szerdel. I had thought I shouldn't go to the camp, as I was studying for an important exam, but a counsellor begged me to come and my aunt to let me go. At camp the custom was that on one day, all the counsellors disappeared. The campers had to choose one girl and one boy to be in charge of the camp for that day. I was the girl who was chosen. I was made to believe I was pretty; I had blond, wavy hair and blue eyes. I thought I was chubby, but I probably was only pleasantly plump. Wherever I went — the Zionist club, school dances — there was always some boy who paid attention to me. Not only did I have someone to dance with, but people would want to cut in, ask to take me home. This was the style in those days.

Finally, in September 1946, I went to the *gimnázium,* which had been my heart's desire for so long. There, too, I became a top student, learning Latin, Hebrew and English, among many other subjects. One of my classmates was Judit Vas. We were not friends at that time, but many years later we declared to each other that we were like sisters. But that is a story for later. When I started the *gimnázium,* I stopped going to the Zionist club because I got busy with other things, such as the private English lessons I was taking.

During this time, we must have been fairly poor. I had no money, and my aunt Malvin was a widow. Aunt Bözsi once took me to a place where I could pick out two pieces of clothing that had been donated from an American organization, I guess for people in need. As a war orphan, I got some allowance from the government; I also got some scholarship money because I did well in school, but not very much. I actually received a certificate of poverty, which I still have. I eventually earned some money from tutoring, and Bözsi took me to buy a white see-through plastic raincoat, which was fashionable at the time. Aunt Ibi and I went to buy shoes, finally — expensive brown platform ones, also out of my own money. I was so proud of that. It meant a lot to me.

One day I went to the Jewish organization we called the Joint to get my school books (I was getting them free because I was an orphan), and somebody approached me and asked me if I wanted to go to America. I said no. I felt that I couldn't tell my aunt Malvin that I wanted to leave. When I went to see my grandparents, my aunt Bözsi was there and I told them what happened. Bözsi said, why not? So that got me thinking about it.

Another day, someone who I think was a social worker came to our apartment and asked if I wanted to go to Canada. At that point, having considered it, I said yes. I was told that I would be adopted and would be able to go to school, and was given the impression that I would live the life of a princess. I was still sick, recovering from paratyphoid, which had caused me to be out of school for three months, and I had to go get a passport photograph taken. My face in that photo looks very drawn and thin, not at all like my usual self.

Eventually I recovered and went back to school, finishing the fifth year of *gimnázium*, which is approximately Grade 9 in North America. During the summer of 1948, when I was fifteen, I went for a holiday with Aunt Malvin and my maternal grandparents in Hajdúszoboszló, a very nice resort. While there, I received a telegram to return home immediately because I was to leave for Canada very shortly.

My aunts Malvin and Ilus did not want me to leave. Ilus tried to bribe me by promising me things if I stayed. They had a piano, and Marika, my younger cousin, had been getting lessons. My uncle Lajos had paid for me to get lessons as well, and I had been practising piano, which I loved. My aunt Ilus said she would buy me a piano if I stayed. But what was a piano in comparison to the princess-like life I was promised in Canada? What could my aunt get me to equal that?

I felt like I actually blackmailed them to let me leave by saying that I did not want to stay in the rotten country where such horrible things had been allowed to happen to us. To this, they had no comeback.

And so I left. My grandparents did not even know I was leaving. I had three grandparents still, at that time. I claimed I wanted to spare them the painful goodbyes, but probably I wanted to spare myself. I was only fifteen years old. After I left Budapest for Canada, I received letters from them often, even though at that time, during the Communist regime, it was dangerous to keep ties with "the West." They apologized for their letters not being interesting, as they led very simple lives. They were also poor. Later on, when we could, my husband and I sent money regularly to help them out. Probably not enough.

Things were just not the same in my family after the war. Beloved members of the family were gone — my parents, uncle Géza, Malvin's husband and extended family. Melanie *néni*, the mother of my second cousin, Helga, had died of starvation in the ghetto. Melanie, sweet but helpless, had lived with my mother and me for a time, and I found hearing about her death very disturbing. She taught me songs that I still remember. Also, there were bad feelings about items that members of my family had left with my non-Jewish uncle. Of course, many material things were lost. But my uncle was also robbed. His house, which was unharmed during the siege, was taken over by a Russian captain and his staff. The family was relegated to the lower level of the house, where I stayed with them right after the liberation. The Russians had felt free to help themselves to anything whatsoever. I don't know what they took.

Before I left Budapest, my aunt Ibi brought my new baby cousin, Kati, with her when she came to say goodbye to me. This was Ibi's second child — she had been pregnant during the war and had my cousin Robi after liberation (on the very day, as we found out much later, that my mother died). Then she had another daughter, Tunde, a few years after Kati's birth.

When my train was leaving, my aunt Malvin ran after it, crying inconsolably. This I was told much later, by my cousin Frici Funk. He told me he was jealous because it seemed that she loved me more than her own daughter, Ági.

I left my family without realizing what step I was actually taking. I took a train with a group of other orphans through Vienna to Paris, where we stayed for several days. In Paris I lived with Frici's (Fred's) sister, Szeren Csillag, and her family. While I was there, they received a telegram from Malvin asking them to hold me back from leaving, at any price. But Szeren's husband told me about the telegram and allowed me to decide my own fate, and I still chose to leave.

No Turning Back

Very soon after I arrived in Vegreville, Alberta, I realized that it was not the place for me. I was totally out of my sphere and experiencing culture shock, and I was very unhappy and lonely. I felt that this life was not what I had been promised by the Canadian Jewish Congress, who was in charge of my care. I wanted to go to Toronto to be with the group of children I had come with from Budapest to Canada. I became very close to some girls I was corresponding with, and especially with Stephen Nasser. Mrs. Klein even teased me about his last name, that it meant "wet" in Yiddish, which I didn't know as I couldn't speak Yiddish. I longed and yearned with all my heart to go to Toronto, to unite with my friends, the only people I knew from my home. And I didn't stop begging and agitating toward that goal.

But what happened was that at the end of the summer of 1949, a year to the day that I arrived in Canada, the Congress finally acquiesced to my pleas: I was able to get on a train and leave Vegreville. I arrived in Winnipeg with the hope of continuing on to Toronto, but Winnipeg would turn out to be the end of my journey — I think it was too expensive for the Congress to send me to Toronto. At the time I still felt like, what am I doing here? But circumstances were such that I decided to stay and go to school.

In Winnipeg, I lived with the Lipkin family — Esther and David and their sons, Raymond and Victor — and went to school at St. John's

Tech in an accelerated Grade 11 class, while working for my room and board. I had a very hard time, going to school and working. I got up, made beds, fed Raymond and Victor breakfast, went to school and came home for lunch to feed the boys; after school, I hoped to study a little bit (having been in Canada only a year, and having skipped Grade 10, I needed to). But then I would get a call to do whatever — prepare supper, do the dishes, babysit, iron the clothes. Saturdays I worked at Adrienne's, a ladies' clothing store owned by the Lipkins; Sunday was cleaning day. I literally didn't have enough time to go to the bathroom.

Esther always introduced me to her friends as her daughter, but I was miserable and lonesome. I worked at the Lipkins' as a slave, I felt. I had to do everything, and it was really too much for a young girl, especially one who hadn't been expected to do housework or do things in the kitchen before. I was actually seriously looking into returning home, preparing documents to be able to return to Hungary and be among my loving family. I felt that I had no one here who loved me, and I loved no one. Stephen and I had eventually stopped corresponding. When I finally heard from him about the possibility of him coming and he asked me to inquire about a job for him and look for a place for him to live near me, I felt that it would be too much of a commitment. Truly, we had barely spent any time with each other, and I had my doubts that we could make it work, considering how young we both were.

At least I had my very good friend Lusia, whom I spent a lot of time with. She was from Poland, and I had first met her when I was taken to Calgary during Christmas of 1948, with the Edmonton orphans. It was supposed to be a treat, I guess. We met all the young people who had come from Europe, as we had, including, to my happiness, Ibi Bein, who was from Budapest and had gone to the same school as me, the Jewish *gimnázium*, but was a year ahead of me. My second cousin Helga was here for a while as well, but we always had a love-hate relationship. She wanted to control me, and I was too headstrong myself and I wouldn't allow for that. She kept saying we would go to Montreal together, but that never happened.

Lusia appeared in Winnipeg at about the same time I did. We were happy to discover each other, to have someone we knew from before. She went to school and worked for her room and board and babysat, as I did, at a family named the Probers. We were in the same class as well.

In the spring of 1950 came the well-known flood. We lived east of Main, on Machray Street, near the Red River. Esther was a total wreck and decided to leave the city with her sons (as many other people did) but left her "daughter" behind. Now I became a refugee again, a flood refugee.

During the flood, I was placed with a family named Blumes. Edith and Wolf Blumes were good to me, and they provided me with room and board and didn't ask me for anything in return. I ate there, and I was mostly free to come and go. School was closed for a while and I worked full-time at Adrienne's for twelve dollars a week. Even though I was paid a pittance, it was still money I wouldn't have had otherwise.

Having become a flood refugee, strangely, things changed for the better. I liked living with the Blumes, and I eventually met a boy I really liked and he seemed to like me too. That made a tremendous change in my life, to like somebody and be liked in return. It meant the world in the mind of a sixteen-year-old romantic, love-starved girl. Life became a little more interesting.

I had met this boy, Harry, through another job I got. Once, when I was visiting Lusia, we wanted some chips, so I rode on my bicycle to get some on Salter Street, at a greasy spoon owned by Lucy and Dave. They asked me if I knew someone who wanted to work there, to help them out. They were very nice to me and the job was okay — serving the customers was not all that hard, and I knew most of them and they were mostly Jewish. Two young men came in one day, and I think both of them asked to take me home. I said okay to the one I thought better looking. But as soon as I had a conversation with that one, I thought he was an idiot. Lucy and Dave knew the other one and also knew his family. They were telling me what a nice boy he was and what a nice family he came from. So I let him take me home the next time he asked. That decision sealed my destiny. He was Harry Garfinkel, a medical student. Our relationship gave me the incentive to decide to remain in Winnipeg. I believed Harry was someone I could rely on.

Around this time, I also had a dream that I was on a boat going home and realized that there was no turning back. When I woke up, I knew that I couldn't do it. I couldn't go back to Hungary. I decided that I would stick it out.

I had another dream around this time, in which I was walking and searching for a place. I knew what the place was. It was Gödöllő, where my great-aunt, my grandmother's sister, lived in the summers, and where I spent time as a child. There was a cherry tree there that I gaily climbed to pick the cherries. I would eat some and throw some to my mother. It was an idyllic memory. Maybe it was also too idyllic a life, since it eventually turned into a nightmare. After waking up, I knew, once again, that I needed to make a life here in Canada.

I went back to school to finish the year. I did not concentrate on studying hard for my final exams, as at that point I was more interested in going out with Harry. But I passed Grade 11 and graduated. The Lipkins had returned and were now leaving for Los Angeles, where her sister had moved. Esther asked me to go with them, but I said no. I was enjoying spending time with Harry, and I wasn't going back to a life of babysitting and working for my room and board. Though they were not moving yet, I decided to do things my way. Nobody was telling me to leave the Blumes. Mrs. and Mr. Blumes were very nice and they had a son about my age.

I decided I wanted to work as much as I could in the summer and save up money and try to go back to school in the fall. So I started looking for jobs. I found one at the Paulin Chambers confectionary factory, on the assembly line. I hated it. I worked for about two weeks or so and then I called in sick; I couldn't make myself return. Some people I spoke with had worked there for decades, but I couldn't see myself doing it.

I knew some people who had opened a dry cleaning and tailor shop and they hired me to be at the desk, taking in clothes, dealing with people, and so on. They paid me less than minimum wage. She was a very pleasant woman; he was friendly, too friendly (he would tell me about his sexual exploits). They spoke Hungarian, and I think they were from Transylvania. I worked in that establishment six days a week. At that time, most people worked half days on Wednesdays. Once, when I wanted to do something, I asked for that afternoon off. When I was refused, I quit.

I met Harry when he had just come back from Portland, Oregon. He had given up dentistry and had been accepted into medical school on the condition that he take a course needed to complete his pre-med requirements. I began to see him every Saturday night and for coffees in between. We didn't go steady, as he still had to go through medical school. So I went out with different boys as well, whom I seemed to meet at different places, such as the YMHA. One boy I had met, Sid, had been away for the summer, I think in Calgary for a job at the stampede. When he came back, he asked me to go to a party with him, and I agreed. But by then I liked Harry so much that I stood Sid up, which wasn't very nice of me. He was very angry with me and let me know in no uncertain terms in a phone call.

After Harry and I had gone out for three years, we got engaged. Subsequently, I was invited to the Garfinkels' house for dinner every single night and they became my family. Harry's sister, Faye, was married to Arnold Tennenhouse and they had an adorable little daughter, Selma, and I bragged about how smart she was to everybody. When Faye had another baby, Carol, I stayed in their house to help out while she was in the hospital. Even though the Tennenhouses have lived in Ottawa for many years, we are still very close. Faye has always said I am her sister. We had a rapport from the beginning. I could talk to her, which I found difficult to do with most people. And I am exceptionally close to Carol. We have long conversations about everything every once in a while.

In the meantime, during the late summer of 1950, I persuaded my friend Lusia to rent a room with me and give up working for our room and board in someone else's home. We found a room in the attic of a house on Magnus Avenue with the Kussins — Lena and Abe and their children, Annette and Dennis. The Kussins had come to Winnipeg from Poland before the war. Abe worked in a factory and Lena took care of the children. They obviously were not well off — they wouldn't have rented their attic if they were.

Harry lived on Burrows Avenue, just a block away. The first drive he took me on was to St. Boniface, where his family used to live when he was younger. His parents had a grocery store here and they lived behind it.

I had two jobs that summer because I was trying to save money in order to be able to go back to school. Harry talked me out of it, advising that it would be too difficult to go to university and also make enough money to live on. In my heart, I agreed with him. I listened to him, deciding to go to business college instead. While we were married, I always joked that he owed me a university degree (which I did get, two in fact). The Canadian Jewish Congress would pay for the tuition, but I had to support myself.

In the fall, both Lusia and I went to a business college called the Manitoba Technical Institute (now called Red River College) during the day. After school and on weekends we both worked at a drugstore on the corner of Burrows Avenue and Salter Street to be able to pay for our room and for our food. The pharmacist was Irv Wiseman, whom I knew because he was a friend of the Lipkins. The job was okay, as people around the neighbourhood came in, including many young people I knew or got to know.

I finished the material at business college quickly, but as per the rules I had to wait for a six-month period to receive my diploma. I was anxious to get a decent job and to make a living. Working for my room and board while going to high school, and then going to business college and working to support myself, had been very hard for me.

In the dead of winter, I went for an interview at Sherwin-Williams paint store, located east of Main on Sutherland Avenue, walking a long distance after I got off the streetcar on Main Street. I was sure it was an effort made in vain. They were known not to hire Jews, and I was also an immigrant, barely here for two years, and to top it off, from behind the Iron Curtain. But I assured the interviewer that I had the confidence to do the job, and I got it!

I worked there for four years until I quit when I was pregnant with my first child. I learned all the tasks that the young women did in that office so that I could substitute for them when they went on holidays. I also made a lifelong friendship with Phyllis Docksteader Anderson, who had gone to the same college as I had. We spent our lunch hours, coffee breaks, and any spare time we had talking and talking. Her family would invite me to dinner and made me feel welcome. I very much enjoyed seeing a normal family sitting down to dinner. Phyllis had a younger sister, Joan, and lovely parents. I knew about Phyllis's first date with Wally, who would become her husband, and I remember how excited she was when she met him. I was her bridesmaid and she was mine. Phyllis lives in Edmonton, and I am still in touch with her.

After living in the attic of the Kussins' home for a while, it was decided that Lusia would find another place to live. It was not possible for us to share a room anymore. I had become very attached to the Kussins, so I was the one who stayed on. In fact, they became like my family, as I had none here.

Lena's brother and the Kussins had decided to buy a dry cleaners' and tailor shop on Corydon Avenue, called Crust Furriers and Tailors. When they moved to Corydon Avenue, I moved with them. They really felt like family then. I ate all my meals with them. They charged me very little for my room — I am sure they didn't make a penny off me. The problem for me became that I was at the other end of the city from my friends and Harry. When we lived close to each other, we could go out for coffee during the week at least, but now that was not possible. Nobody had cars either. So I decided to move back to the North End. I found a room on Boyd and Salter with Mr. and Mrs. Kreman, a very nice older Jewish couple who were childless. They liked me enough and were also very nice to me, but their home wasn't my home — I just rented the one small room where I lived. After a while they provided me dinner, for which I paid. I liked coming back from work and having my dinner waiting. I wasn't allowed to use the kitchen. Mrs. Kreman was extremely clean, and I heard from Lena that she complained that I didn't wipe the bathtub. But by then, none of this really mattered. In 1953, Harry and I were engaged, and we would be getting married the following year.

My friend Kathy Blum Griesz hosted a wedding shower for me. When I was opening a gift given to me by Harry's mother, a set of cutlery, all of a sudden I could not stop crying. One of the guests asked Kathy why I was crying. She said it was because I didn't have my parents with me as I was getting married. Kathy, who was also a survivor and a war orphan from Hungary, understood me.

On June 19, 1954, the night before our wedding, we were working on the table settings till late in the evening. When Harry took me home he gave me a sleeping pill so I could have a good night's sleep and be well rested on the day of the wedding. Early in the morning Mrs. Kreman woke me up because a congratulations telegram came for me and I had to sign for it. She wasn't very smart — she could have signed for it! I was awakened from a deep sleep, not having slept off the sleeping pill. I phoned Harry who sent Isaac, his younger brother, over with a pill to keep me awake. I was under the influence of this pill all day! I wasn't hungry, I couldn't eat, and I think I was a little more lively than I would have been normally....

At the wedding, both the Kussins and the Kremans sat at my side of the head table. I had actually asked Abe Kussin to walk me down the aisle and give me away, but Harry's father wanted to, which was a little strange, I thought. But they paid for the wedding because I certainly couldn't, and I had very few guests to invite, as well. I gave my husband, Harry, my father's wedding band, which my father had left behind. Harry later lost the ring, a carelessness that upset me very much. My mother didn't leave her wedding band because she thought she would survive.

After we got married, Harry started interning at St. Boniface Hospital, but he was still not making any money in those days. I was still working, of course. While working, I saved as much money as I could. I wanted to contribute as much as possible to our future. So I paid for the furniture when we got married.

We rented an upstairs apartment in a private house on Boyd, with the Millers. We had only one hundred dollars in the bank, and Harry decided he wanted to buy a TV. He was working long hours as an intern and said it was for me. I said I didn't want it because I didn't want to spend our last penny on a television, but he insisted he wanted to buy it for me and did. Naturally, having our first TV was amazing. Up until that time we had watched at Faye's, or my in-laws.

Harry graduated from medical school in 1955. He worked for a year for the Mall Medical Clinic, which had been founded after the war by two Jewish doctors who had been together in a World War II army hospital. I remember all of them, even though Harry was with them only for one year. They were very nice, but they had a very strong influence on him. Harry was interested in becoming an obstetrician, and I felt I should let him do as he wished. But Dr. Ruvin Lyons told him, "Son, don't do it," and he also told that to his son, and they both took radiology.

Harry applied to a different hospital for residency in radiology. He was accepted in different places but understood that the best training available was in Boston at the Beth Israel Hospital (now called the Beth Israel Deaconess Medical Center). The receptionist at the Mall clinic worked on his correspondence with the hospital and she said the pay wasn't too bad for those days, six hundred dollars a month. But in fact, it was a six-hundred-dollar stipend for a year, when our rent for a month in Boston was one hundred dollars! In any case, that was the job Harry accepted. His family promised to help financially, which they did. The stipend was negligible, and his parents really helped us to survive. They also encouraged us to start a family. We couldn't have a baby without knowing that they would help us. Our adorable baby girl, Gail, was born on November 23, 1955, and was delivered by Dr. Lyons.

Before we left for Boston the next year, we changed our names from Garfinkel to Garfield, with the full approval of Harry's father. In mid-1956, Harry took up residence in radiology. It wasn't an easy time financially, but not bad on the whole. There were many positive things about living in Boston. In that apartment house were several young couples all in the same or very similar financial position we were in. Most were receiving help from parents; others would run short at the end of the month. We never went out for dinner, but we went to the theatre a lot, buying the cheapest tickets. And I would go on the streetcar to Filene's Basement to shop for bargains. One of our friends had a car, and she often took us to the beach, and in the evenings, I sometimes went to a book club.

I had an exceptionally good friend in the building, Anne Kahan (her husband was from Transylvania I think), and we talked and talked about everything. But when we left Boston, we didn't continue our friendship. And I had my adopted sister Judit Vas (Judy Wolf), whom I had found serendipitously. Or rather, Harry had.

In 1957 or so, Harry met a fellow resident who had a familiar accent. He turned out to be from Hungary, and he and his wife had left during the Hungarian Revolution. So they set to exchanging information and discovered that their wives were the same age. When they asked for maiden names and brought them home to show us, it turned out that we had been classmates in the *gimnázium*! This started a wonderful and long friendship between Judy and me, which lasted until she died. In my last call to her I addressed her as my sister. When her son Rob called me to tell me that she'd died, I was thunderstruck. But what can one do against the inevitable? We have to accept all that comes our way. I really miss her.

~

I wanted to have another baby, and I was really hoping for a boy. I guess it was still in my mind, my father apparently wanting a boy, and also, I wanted to please my in-laws, who had three granddaughters. In any case, I became pregnant. For nine months I drove Harry crazy. He had to check the baby's heartbeat and try to guess from that what it might mean. But of course, there was no way to know. If it was faster, the baby might be smaller, which might mean it was a girl? Who knew?

Our son was born in Boston on June 27, 1957, and was named David Bernard after my father, Bernat. I was thrilled to have a son, but it was really hard to have two babies. Gail was only nineteen months when David was born, and she didn't yet sleep through the night. Fortunately, David was an excellent baby. He slept a lot and rarely cried.

During the 1956 Hungarian Revolution, several of my cousins had left Hungary and were stranded in Austria. Harry's family — his father and sister — sponsored them, and three sets of my relatives arrived in Winnipeg. I cannot express how happy I was. It was unbelievable, really. I now had family, my own flesh and blood, living in Canada! It is important to mention that I was a real orphan, having no family whatsoever on this continent aside from my distant cousin, Helga. One family that came was the Funks — my cousin Ági, her husband, Fred (previously known as Frici), and their children, Kathy and George. Ági is my cousin by blood, six years older than me, my aunt Malvin's daughter. The second family, the Osztermanns, consisted of my cousin Bandi, his wife, Edith, and their daughter, Susan. The child was supposedly named after me, because she was born in 1949, after I left. The third family was the Acels, consisting of my cousin Éva, who was four years older than me, and her husband, Frank. Some of my family told me that my grandmother had really wanted them to come, that she had almost insisted, because I was here all alone. My aunt Malvin was also eventually able to come and that was really wonderful because I loved her, and she was as close to a mother to me as was possible. Sadly, she died of breast cancer a long time ago, in 1967, and since then the family hasn't been as close. She was a wise, smart, wonderful person.

After three years in Boston, we returned to Winnipeg for a wedding, and Dr. McLaughlin offered Harry a position. The salary, twelve thousand dollars, sounded heavenly. I didn't know what we were going to do with all the money he was going to earn (it turned out it was no problem spending that much a year!). We had always planned on coming back to Winnipeg to live because of Harry's family, even though by that time, Faye and Arnold had moved to Ottawa.

We bought a house, my first, on Primrose Avenue with help from my in-laws. It was a small house, but it pleased me a great deal. And it was unbelievably satisfying to me to have family there. They were all very good to me when I returned from Boston with the children and Harry was still in Boston for a short time, finishing up a locum. Through my family I also met all the other Hungarian Jews who had come to Winnipeg after the Revolution. Until then, they were very few and far between.

In 1959, Harry was working very long hours. He also had to study, as he still had to write exams to qualify as a radiologist. He didn't have very much time to spare. I was able to get a babysitter sometimes and have some time of my own. Gail was a blond, blue-eyed, little beauty. David had his father's dark hair, full lips and blue eyes, but a baby picture of mine shows that he looked exactly like me at that age!

When we lived on Primrose, Gail went to the I.L. Peretz Folk School, which was close by. A private nursery school was there, too, to which we sent David. At that point I was seriously considering finding ways to continue my education, which had always been my wish. There was no mature education program as yet, where you could go to university without having completed high school. So in 1962, with great willpower, I started going to night school at St. John's Tech, my old school, where I had gone for Grade 11. And coincidentally, my old principal, Mr. Reeve, was teaching the world history course!

I had gotten pregnant before I started going back to school. I definitely wanted to have another child, but nothing was going to stop me from continuing to attend that class. So I attended up to the time of my delivery and returned to class as soon as I could after giving birth. I got a lot of attention then, everybody asking me about the baby, Shelley. She was absolutely adorable. A small baby, a bit premature, she had a perfectly round little head and was beautiful from the start. She is named after my paternal grandmother, whose Hebrew name is Rachel. Harry didn't like the name Rachel and I didn't like Rochelle. I suggested we name her Rochelle but call her Shelley. Harry said that if we call her Shelley, we name her Shelley. And so it was. I discussed it, of course, with my mother-in-law, who liked the name. She told me that "*sheli*" means "mine" in Hebrew, which I knew.

The date of Shelley's birth was February 27, 1962. When we came home from the hospital my in-laws came to see her. I remember my father-in-law putting on and tying my mother-in-law's boots. She was very sick with angina and had to spend most of her time in bed. She died very shortly after. We were glad that at least she was able to see her new granddaughter.

I then decided that in order to complete Grade 12, I would attend half days at Garden City Collegiate because we lived very close to the school. I was often told I could pass for one of the students. In 1963, at twenty-nine years old, I finally graduated from high school.

Dreams and Losses

In 1964, Harry and I went to London, England, to interview Dr. Hope for Harry's new practice. It hadn't taken Harry that long to quit working for Dr. McLaughlin, and he soon started to work for himself. He worked extremely hard to build up a practice, which he did very successfully. He eventually had enough work to have three partners. As he got more help, we were able to travel quite a bit.

From London, we made plans to fly to Budapest, as I had wanted to go back home. These were still the days of the Iron Curtain, and it felt like the plane was spiriting us away to Hungary. But we made it, and then I was in Budapest, where we were treated royally. I went back to all my old haunts, which was an interesting experience. Unfortunately, my beloved grandparents weren't alive anymore, but many other people from my past were, including my friend Suzie Löwy. I still had a lot of family there, including my two aunts on my father's side, Bözsi and Berta. I also went to see my old neighbours, several of whom still lived in the same apartment building I grew up in. Then we went to the apartment where I used to live, and the current resident let us come in. In that apartment, where I had lived with my parents, and later only my mother, from ages three to eleven, when the Arrow Cross took my mother away, I totally broke down, unable to stop myself from crying uncontrollably, for the second time in my life.

My cousin Éva and her husband, Frank, were also visiting Budapest at this time. They had a car and were driving to Vienna, so we went with them, with the goal of finding where my mother was buried. Frank drove us around, trying to find Neudörfl, which was not easy because it is a small place and we didn't speak much German. We finally did manage to find it. Three Hungarian Jewish women had been buried at the outskirts of the Roman Catholic cemetery. Their deaths were registered officially. I had a memorial plaque made to take there the next time we visited the gravesite. But when Harry went to make inquiries at the appropriate Jewish organization, we found out that the bodies had been exhumed by the Jewish community and reburied in the Jewish cemetery in the city of Eisenstadt.

~

In 1965, we were able to buy a big lot and build a beautiful house at 426 Kelvin Boulevard. The children changed schools, and Gail started attending the Ramah Hebrew School. And I finally started achieving my dream: university. By this point in our lives, while I was taking university classes and bringing up my children, we could afford to hire somebody to help me around the house.

Harry was still working very long hours and kept busy. I went to the University of Winnipeg and naturally, the first course I registered for was psychology. As I was listening to the prof, I doubted that I was university material. I couldn't understand what he was talking about. I spoke about this to my sister-in-law, Esther, who had graduated from the same university. She suggested I transfer to a different prof's course, at which point everything changed and became clear. I majored in psychology, then did the honours program in philosophy. At first, I took just one course a year, then increased to two, then three. I registered for some subjects that were of interest to me — English literature, for example, which I had been afraid to take previously, English not being my first language. I enjoyed every aspect of my classes. I felt stimulated going to lectures and made some friends along the way. My goal was to satisfy and expand my mind, not work toward a career. In 1975, I received my degree, a bachelor of arts (honours). That year, I also received a Gold Medal in philosophy. I felt very good about that.

I was also doing some other things in my life. Harry and I often went to the theatre, the Royal Winnipeg Ballet, football games and hockey games, and I was very active physically, running and playing tennis. I aimed to do whatever I set my mind to do, well. I have some tennis trophies from those years, and I also ran a marathon. Originally, I had no intention of completing it, but I just kept going until I did. I surprised even myself. I believe I was a good and understanding mother, more so because I kept active.

After I graduated from university, I was looking for something to do. I thought perhaps I ought to consider a career, something that would help me get a decent job and earn some money. After some career counselling, I registered for the Recreation Studies program at the University of Manitoba.

I was good at both academic and physical activities, especially gymnastics. I had always been very good at gymnastics — as a child I had gotten tips from my father's cousin Jeno, who was a professional acrobat. So gymnastics was the first course I took in the Recreation Studies program. At forty-two years old I could do all the requirements that were expected from the eighteen-year-olds in that class. That was an experience! I also learned to cross-country ski, another required activity. I didn't especially enjoy many of the course requirements, but I did them in order to get the degree.

I then got a job teaching swimming at the YMHA. I found the conditions and people comfortable, although the pay was negligible. But that didn't matter so much to me. In addition to swimming, I taught water exercise classes and fitness classes. I wasn't expected to teach those classes, but I had taken the qualifying training to be able to, and I wanted to know that I could teach these activities the right way. I enjoyed being there, and I stuck with the job until 1997, when the Y moved to a new location and became known as the Rady Centre.

When we reached the stage in our lives when Harry could work fewer hours, take holidays and have a more comfortable, stress-free life, lightning struck. Or maybe it was more like thunder. He became depressed. I vacillated about mentioning or including this in my memoirs, but I am writing about my life, and this matter did deeply affect my life. At a time when it is known how widespread and common mental illness is, it should be freely discussed, not be a hush-hush matter. And I have realized how deeply and profoundly depression affects not only the individual, but also the whole family.

Harry still went to work, but after work he would go to bed and had no energy or desire to do anything else. I couldn't understand it. I told him that he had absolutely everything to feel good about — our life was perfect: his work situation, his family life, his children, everything. But of course, this made no difference to him. This situation went on for a while, maybe several weeks, and it had to be kept secret because if it got out, his professional life would be in danger.

And then he emerged from this state and became more energetic. Very energetic, in fact. He was often this way before a planned holiday. As his depressed states turned into energetic ones, his state of mind became more frantic. I knew things were desperately wrong, but he refused to seek help for fear of hurting his reputation as a doctor. I tried to enlist the help of his partners but they were less than sympathetic.

Eventually he agreed to see a psychiatrist in Ottawa, arranged by his family there. He did get some medication, but it didn't really work. By this time it was clear to me that he had bipolar disorder and I said so. A family member asked me how I could diagnose him. Well, it was very easy. We were in Mexico when things really got out of hand. He didn't sleep and was constantly shopping, and I was almost out of my mind with worry and fear. I didn't know how I would get him on the plane to get home.

Harry bought so much stuff in Mexico that the authorities kept us at the airport in Winnipeg for hours. He was like a raging bull there, pacing back and forth. Finally I said to someone in charge, "Can't you see this man is sick?" So they let us go home. For a while I kept a list of all the stuff he bought in Mexico, to assure myself that I wasn't the one who was crazy.

Harry did go to see a psychiatrist in Winnipeg, and he was pre-scribed an antidepressant when he was low and other medication when high. Eventually his highs were spectacular, and I knew in my soul that something wasn't right. Along with him, the whole fam-ily was going through hell. He would buy expensive and unwanted things, and then my son would try to return them. This situation especially affected my two younger children who were still living at home.

Finally, Harry agreed to check into a hospital in Chicago to be helped. For some reason, he decided to go to the office just before he left, and he found that he had been locked out. What a shock it was to his system, and to the whole family, is impossible to measure. It is a testimony to his desire to get well that he managed to carry on with the plan to go to Chicago and check into the hospital. There he was put on a regimen of medication, which, finally, managed to stabilize him. After that time, our lives became more peaceful and serene. He parted ways with his partners and some of his clients stayed with him.

I need to add that many of his friends stayed away after his break-down, though some colleagues who were loyal were willing to cover for him if he got sick or we went on holiday. His being seriously ill and deprived of his work put me and the whole family in a state of great stress, to express it mildly. He also got himself into debt with his buying sprees and careless spending, which is a very real symptom of a person in a manic stage.

After Harry was stabilized, he became a calm and quiet person, much less energetic than he had been previously. But mentally he was as good as ever and never relapsed. From that time on, Harry worked on his own, half days, which worked out just fine, considering his all-around health and his age. He did that to the very day he died, suddenly, of a heart attack on November 30, 1994. He had had different heart problems, as well as diabetes, but his death was still very unexpected. Later, I remembered that Harry would excuse himself when he got very tired. I guess that should have been a sign of some weakness. Still, his death was a great shock for us all, and it was extremely devastating.

However, Harry was able to attend all his children's weddings and enjoy and take pride in four of his grandchildren. We used to have Shabbat dinners, and the whole family would be together. Those evenings were always very wonderful.

In 1976, when Gail was twenty-one, she married David Halbrich from Israel. They have two brilliant children, Michelle and Alon. In 1983, Shelley, also at age twenty-one, married David Youssiem. They have two lovely, talented daughters, Lauren and Ashley. And in May 1994, David married Carole Solomon. They have two gorgeous and clever boys, Hart and Matthew. My family has been the smartest thing I have accomplished in my whole life. Now I also have one beautiful great-granddaughter, Lia, and a charismatic great-grandson, Evan. What more can a grandmother ask for?

Michelle is a pediatric allergist. Alon is an actuary, married, with two children. In 1994, Alon was learning his Haftorah, and Harry and I often heard him practice. But Harry died before Alon's actual bar mitzvah. Lauren, Shelley's daughter, was born in 1990. We could observe her creative talents at a very early age, and when she got older, she went to Toronto to pursue fashion design. Ashley just graduated and is working as an occupational therapist.

Harry never knew David and Carole's beautiful boys, Hart and Matthew, which is very sad, as he would have greatly enjoyed them and loved them. Hart just graduated from university. He is excellent in math, just like his father. Mathew is still a student, and he works as well. He is very industrious, as are all my grandchildren and my children. My children always had jobs. They never expected a handout, even though we could have afforded to give them enough pocket money for them to manage. I always believed earned money was more meaningful and more appreciated. I also allowed them to learn to be very independent. They were not driven everywhere; they had to take the bus instead. They speak about that often. I hope they don't resent that. I believe that is how they became the amazingly independent and self-reliant human beings they are.

When Harry died, I was still working at the YMHA, and it helped a great deal to go back to work and have something to do. Time goes on. Everyone was busy in my family, working or going to school. All my children received the education they desired. And I have been able to oversee all that. Unfortunately, their father could not. He would have loved to see his grandchildren thrive, or at least be at their respective bar and bat mitzvahs.

Three years after Harry's death, I met and married Harvey Allen, someone I had known for a long time and whom I respected as a human being. We had a few nice years of travelling, and we spent winters in Palm Springs. We were happy and we enjoyed a very pleasant social life — there were Friday night dinners I made for my family, which Harvey enjoyed being part of, and dinners at the homes of his sons.

Harvey and I also went to Israel to visit his daughter and her family who lived on a kibbutz. I discovered that a cousin of my mother's, Alfred Herschkowitch, had moved to Israel from Romania (previously the area known as Transylvania, which was part of Hungary during the war). I remembered when he came to Budapest during the war; he was a very young man at the time, and I was a child. While we were in Israel, Alfred and his family invited us for lunch, and afterwards, Harvey left us for a while so that we could visit properly, since my family and I conversed in Hungarian. That visit is very memorable for me. Alfred's wife, Ági, died a while later and I stayed in touch with Alfred and his family.

Then Harvey suffered a stroke, and life became extremely stressful, on account of many issues I won't go into. However, we managed and tried to make the best of things. Sadly, Harvey got cancer and passed away in 2004.

I was brave enough to try again and I had a very nice and good relationship with my third husband, Herb Halprin. We had a good few years together until, sadly, he developed Alzheimer's disease. At the end, he didn't remember much, but what he did remember was his mother and me. I looked after him and took care of problems and situations to the best of my abilities. I didn't give up on anybody. I survived all that as well. Herb passed away in 2014.

What was most difficult to get through was the untimely death of my beloved son-in-law, David, Shelley's husband, in 2016. He was diagnosed with colon cancer, and he died far, far too young, His death affected my whole family. I used to call us the House of David, as both my sons-in-law and my son are named David. And we greatly miss the missing one. It is impossible to describe the shock and sadness in the wake of that event. I don't know how it is possible to recover from such a blow. I know my daughter and granddaughters live under this shadow. But life must go on somehow and it does. I know that as well as anybody.

Reunions

Throughout the years, I kept in touch with the Kleins, the people I had lived with in Vegreville. After Harry died, my friend Phyllis Anderson invited me to visit her and her family in Edmonton. While I was there, one of Mr. Klein's daughters-in-law (Hymie's wife) arranged for me to visit him. Phyllis took me to the apartment and wanted to leave me there, but I asked her to stay. We found Mr. Klein alone in the apartment. I was a bit disappointed, as I had hoped to meet Hymie's wife, whom I had good memories of. (Hymie died very young.) Mr. Klein welcomed us and seemed pleased to see me. We conversed for some time, but after a while I found it a little uncomfortable and difficult to keep up the conversation. I nodded to Phyllis, thinking it was time to leave. She, being the kind soul she is, indicated that I should stay. In trying to think of something to do, I asked him to show me pictures of his grandchildren. He took out an album, and as we were looking through it, he pointed to one photo and announced: "This is my adopted daughter." And the person he pointed to was none other than me.

I was so totally affected that I almost stopped breathing. I realized that he had no idea who I was. He must have had Alzheimer's or dementia. Perhaps he was just glad to see any visitor who came his way. I felt bad for him, but I was most affected by the fact that, in his mind, all along, he had thought of me as his adopted daughter. I almost couldn't believe what I had heard. I cannot describe it, but it was like a blow to my consciousness. I was glad Phyllis was there to witness the incident. Phyllis took pictures of us, and we left with the promise to send some pictures, a promise that I kept. It was some time later that I received a letter from his son Allan. He informed me that Mr. Klein had died and he let me know that he was aware of our visit and that the pictures had been received.

~

After being in Winnipeg for a while and establishing my life here, I had lost touch with my Hungarian friends in Toronto. The longest correspondence I had kept up was with Stephen Nasser, who had even offered to come to Winnipeg. But by then, we hadn't seen each other for so long, and I felt that we were still too young to make a commitment.

But later on, I wondered what had happened to these friends. I would ask everybody who came from Toronto whether they knew anything about them. But nobody knew of the boy with whom I had been corresponding so many years ago, who had even been willing to move to Winnipeg when I couldn't seem to find a way to get to Toronto.

In the mid-2000s, I was with some friends one day, and they asked me to tell them about my background. So I was reminiscing and related to them my tale of woe about a long correspondence with a boy whom I was never able to meet up with, and whom I lost touch with, it appeared, forever. One friend got on the internet, and lo and behold, there was Stephen, larger than life. He was an author, and in 2003 he had written a memoir about his experiences as a young boy, just thirteen years old, who had been taken to Auschwitz-Birkenau. I felt that my first obligation was to read his book and know about his story (I was not aware that he had been in Auschwitz, as it was not a part of our conversations when we spent time together). I ordered his book and read it before getting in touch with his publisher to find out whether Stephen wished to get in touch with me. And indeed he did!

It was a most satisfying conclusion to our story when he and his wife, Françoise, came from Las Vegas to visit Herb and me when we wintered in Palm Springs. We saw them there a few times, and we also visited them in Las Vegas. Stephen is quite an amazing person. He had visited, I believe, over a thousand schools, churches and halls all over the United States as a speaker. He is a very popular, inspirational speaker, not only about his life, but also about democracy, freedom and humanity in general. He is an extremely upbeat, amazing human being. We are still in touch.

I didn't give up on trying to find my other Hungarian friends from long ago, and my persistence paid off. When Phyllis invited me to visit her in Edmonton again, I phoned Judy Edelman, who I knew lived there. She had come with the first group of kids from Hungary and was brought to Winnipeg, where I met her. She then went on to Toronto, met her husband and they decided to go to Edmonton and open the first Jewish bakery there. Judy and I made arrangements to meet for lunch, and I finally had a link to my past. I asked her if she knew another group of kids who were from Hungary and lived in Toronto. I couldn't quite believe my ears when she said she did and gave me the name of a person I remembered very well, her friend Suzie Szilasy. Phone calls immediately took place, which resulted in a wonderful reunion in Toronto in 2007, in Johnny Wagner's home. It was unbelievably amazing. I found it extremely touching and wonderful to be with my old friends, and to see Stephen and Françoise again. Unfortunately, a few of the group had died by then, I was very sorry to hear. Johnny's wife told me that her husband had referred to me over the years as the lost one. It was really overwhelming, the idea that I hadn't been forgotten.

Sometime earlier, I had discovered a documentary on TV called *Children of the Storm* (made by Jack Kuper, in the year 2000). In it, a woman my age was interviewed about her life during the war. What had happened to her parents sounded exactly like what had happened to mine. I wished I could meet her, but I had no idea who she was, and she wasn't identified in the documentary. But when I went to the reunion in Toronto, there she was — Kitty Salsberg! We had been in the same group that came to Canada from Budapest.

~

I also kept in touch with my high school friend Myra Goldstein, who lives in Saskatoon, and my childhood friend Vera Teitelbaum, who lives in New York. Of my friends in Winnipeg, Lusia and Gizi (Ellen) were lifelong ones, and we were in touch until the end of their lives. Lusia had moved to Toronto soon after we finished business college, but we saw each other when we could and we had long conversations over the years about our lives, our families and especially about the books we read. Lusia passed away around 2015. Gizi fell ill many years earlier, and the last time I spoke with her was when she was in the hospital. I told her how much I loved her and what she meant to me. Her husband, Yehoshua, was so kind that he continued to phone me on my birthday for several years afterwards, I think as if in her place.

The other person who was extremely important to me in Winnipeg was Gabriel Kerenyi; he and Ellen were the only ones I knew from home, and the reason I decided I could handle staying in Winnipeg. Gabriel was smart and talented, with a good sense of humour. He and his mother eventually moved to Montreal, and then I heard that he had moved to New York to pursue engineering. Nobody in my group of friends heard from him after that, so we could never find him to invite him to the reunion. Eventually I started searching for news of him online. The information I found was, unfortunately, his obituary. I found out that he was a well-thought-of engineer, beloved father and grandfather, and a talented pianist. I saw also that his original last name, Kohn, which had first been Hungarianized to Kerenyi and then anglicized to Kern, had been changed back to the original, Kohn, on his tombstone. He must have wished for it to be so. Finding his 2015 obituary was a sad, poignant, but somehow satisfying end to his story.

Epilogue

The war orphans, including my friend Ibi Bein and I, were actively sought out and convinced that we would be looked after, adopted, sent to school. My memory of the promise that was made to us, "you will be a princess," is not an exaggeration, but a fact. It was made to both Ibi and me. There was a correspondence to this effect between Ibi's uncle and the Canadian Jewish Congress (CJC). And yet, Ibi was so miserable that I later heard that she had killed herself. She was a good friend of mine, someone I loved and felt kinship with, who was in very much the same circumstances as me, and her death affected me deeply. And it made me question things.

In some sense, I have big regrets. I left everyone I loved and everyone who truly loved and cared for me and grieved for me. I set out for my great adventure, but I was really too immature to understand the full consequences of that decision. And I was also misled. I was told I would be adopted and be able to continue with my schooling, as I certainly would have done had I stayed in Budapest. It took me years to accept the idea that my place was here, and to find my place.

My disappointments and loneliness and a sense of powerlessness in having to fight for myself when I was introduced to my new country made me quite ambivalent. The transition was mean and miserable. I accomplished a lot, learning English and getting accolades for my high marks at school within ten months of my arrival, but with misery. And I went through all that at age fifteen, which is a tough age to get through under "normal" circumstances.

The theme of my life from very early childhood was, "I want to go home," desperately, and with a very strong will I was able to accomplish this whenever I was away from my mother as a child. I mentioned this in my childhood reminiscences, that I would become terribly lonely and desire the comfort of home.

After the war I had my parents no more. But I did have a very warm, very loving family. My grandparents and my aunts, my mother's sisters, adored me. I think they tried extra hard because I lost my parents and they also lost a daughter and sister, and it was as if I was the one left of her. I did feel that made me special to them. It is a bittersweet feeling.

The promise I made myself as a child, never to show a hurt, never to show vulnerability or need, probably helped me survive. But a person needs more than that to survive. I was deprived of life-nourishing love at such a young age: first when I said goodbye to my most beloved father, understanding in my heart that I would never see him again. This is my worst memory from the Holocaust. Then I lost my warm, loving mother. And I persevered. I survived the war, the persecution.

When I had the promise of a wonderful life in North America, my adventurous spirit won out. When I encountered the cold facts of my circumstances there, I yearned for my warm family circle. But I realized, realistically, that it was too late. I was also separated from the group I believe would have been at least substitute family here in Canada. I felt, for the longest time, that there was nobody around me who really loved me — not unconditionally. So I did the best I could. I relied on myself. I finished high school at least, went to business college, supported myself and found love. But until I got married at age twenty-one, I lived alone in a rented room. It was pretty lonely, sometimes overwhelmingly so. Sometimes I took the long way home from work, just to reduce the time I had to be alone in my room.

I believe that my wings were clipped in some way. I did what I had to do to survive, and I bided my time until I was married and had children. In that way, I eventually created a family of my own. When it became possible, I pursued an education, which had been my goal since arriving in Canada, and the reason for my terrible frustration at the beginning of my life here.

I stayed in Winnipeg, and I spent my whole life here; I grew old here. I had a comfortable life and I accomplished many of my goals, though not the way I dreamt I would as an innocent, ignorant young person. I have wonderful, devoted children. All have the qualities most desirable in human beings: to be a mensch, smarts, decency, self-reliance, good looks and more. My children all stayed faithful to their partners and raised good children. They are thoughtful children to their mother. They all married Jewish people, and that was important to me, as well as to their father.

I often think about how my grandchildren exist and have the opportunity to follow their dreams and accomplish in life whatever they are capable of because I managed to stay alive. My parents have descendants they would adore and would be so proud of. When I pass by a photo of one of my grandsons, I think of my father. Whether the resemblance is there or I just imagine it, it doesn't matter. I remember and think of my father and my mother too — my beautiful, young, strong mother, who thought she could survive it all, whose last words I know of were, "I must leave to find my child."

～

You can't go home again. It is true in so many ways. My aunt Malvin told me much later, when she lived here in Winnipeg, that although they would not have discouraged me, when I wrote them of my plans to come home, she knew that I couldn't have gone back to school in Hungary, having been in the West. I would not have been considered the same person as I was before I left — a poor war orphan.

How did I get here? How do I evaluate or assess, sum up and wind up the story of my life? Strength of character. Will to continue. Will to provide immortality for my parents. Will to accomplish my goals, to give meaning to my life. I had a marriage of forty years, which I consider very successful. We loved one another. I fought and worked hard for everything I accomplished here.

One year, on International Women's Day, I received a note from one of my granddaughters. "I look up to you more than you know and I love you very much." And this statement has the power to erase all the bad memories and affirm that my life was more than worth it.

As I age, these are the most poignant years of my life. Yet the fact that I refer to Budapest as home after all these years makes me wonder about my deepest feelings: a deep sense of loneliness, never quite overcome; a sense of wanting to belong, but not quite belonging. Budapest is home in the sense that it was the only time in my life, for a while, for a short time, that I felt safe and loved unconditionally.

I did make some very good friends over the many years I have been living in Canada. The best of those have passed away. At present, my best friends are those old ones from "home" with whom I am still in touch. Recently, I was able to find an image of my childhood home on the internet. Maybe it was merely nostalgia, but when I saw it, I was overwhelmed by the feeling that I never had that kind of home in Canada. How could I? In Budapest, my childhood home was the only time I had my loving parents with me.

And although I believe Canada is the best country in the world, and I am proud to be here and to be Canadian, I often still feel like an immigrant, not totally fitting in or included, like an outsider among friends who grew up together — never as close as I am with someone who has the same past as me or with my old friends. I'm not sure that how I feel now is how I have always felt. But I have written things the way I feel about them now.

What happened to me in the Holocaust, and to others I knew and to those I did not even know, affected me irrevocably. It makes life very precious. I don't take things for granted. I thank God for being alive. I thank God that I have children, not just for myself, but to give meaning and continuity to the life of my parents and thus provide them with a form of immortality through their grandchildren. My children and grandchildren are so precious to me. But my feelings are often bittersweet, joy mingled with pain. Very often when I look at them, I think of other babies and children who died tragically and needlessly. I cannot help imagining the horror of a helpless mother as she realized what was happening to her and her children. And it was perhaps only after I became a parent myself that I realized, not just the extent of my personal losses, but the pain my mother must have felt when she was forced to abandon me in such life-threatening circumstances.

Not many days go by when I don't remember. I especially remember the children, probably because I was, then, a child myself. I remember the little girls in the countryside with whom I was playing when I was ten. I remember the young cousins who lived in Transylvania. None of them survived the war.

Often, a person relating a story from those times might say: I was lucky; if not on account of some small turn of events, I would have been killed. Be it luck or fate, those who took the wrong turn or were in the wrong place at the wrong time cannot be here to tell their story. In the words of Horace, an ancient Roman poet: "Why do you laugh? Change but the name and the story is told of yourself." Why do I cry? Change the name and the story is told of me. And this is why I have told my story — not only because I feel an obligation to tell it, but because in the telling, I remember those who cannot tell their stories.

Glossary

Allies The coalition of countries that fought against the Axis powers (Germany, Italy and Japan, and later others). At the beginning of World War II, in September 1939, the coalition included France, Poland and Britain. After Germany invaded the USSR in June 1941 and the United States entered the war following the bombing of Pearl Harbor by Japan on December 7, 1941, the main leaders of the Allied powers became Britain, the USSR and the United States. Other Allies included Canada, Australia, India, Greece, Mexico, Brazil, South Africa and China. *See also* Axis.

American Jewish Joint Distribution Committee (JDC) Colloquially known as the Joint, the JDC was a charitable organization founded in 1914 to provide humanitarian assistance and relief to Jews all over the world in times of crisis. It provided material support for persecuted Jews in Germany and other Nazi-occupied territories and facilitated their immigration to neutral countries such as Portugal, Turkey and China. Between 1939 and 1944, Joint officials helped close to 81,000 European Jews find asylum in various parts of the world. Between 1944 and 1947, the JDC assisted more than 100,000 refugees living in DP camps by offering retraining programs, cultural activities and financial assistance for emigration.

Arrow Cross Party (in Hungarian, Nyilaskeresztes Párt — Hungarista Mozgalom; abbreviation: Nyilas) A Hungarian right-wing extremist and antisemitic party founded by Ferenc Szálasi in 1935 as the Party of National Will. The newly renamed Arrow Cross Party ran in Hungary's 1939 election and won 15 per cent of the vote. The party was fought and largely suppressed by the regime in the coming years, but re-emerged as a major force in March 1944, when Germany occupied Hungary; in August 1944, the party was temporarily banned. Under Nazi approval, the party, led by Szálasi, assumed control of Hungary from October 15, 1944, to March 28, 1945. The Arrow Cross regime instigated the murder of tens of thousands of Hungarian Jews. Starting on November 6, with the last group leaving on December 11, 1944, approximately 70,000 Jews were rounded up and sent on death marches toward Greater Germany. Tens of thousands died or were murdered along the way, and some 50,000 survivors were handed over to the Germans. Between October 1944 and January 1945, the Arrow Cross murdered thousands of Jews in Budapest. *See also* Budapest ghetto; Szálasi, Ferenc.

Auxiliary Labour Service (Also referred to as forced labour battalions or forced labour service) Units of Hungary's military-related labour service system (in Hungarian, *Munkaszolgálat*), which was first established in 1919 for those considered too "politically unreliable" for regular military service. After the labour service was made compulsory in 1939, Jewish men of military age were recruited to serve; however, having been deemed "unfit" to bear arms, they were equipped with tools and employed in mining, road and rail construction and maintenance work. Though the men were treated relatively well at first, the system became increasingly punitive. By 1941, Jews in forced labour battalions were required to wear an armband and civilian clothes; they had no formal rank and were unarmed; they were often mistreated by extremely antisemitic supervisors; and the work they had to do, such as clearing minefields, was often fatal. By 1942, 100,000 Jewish men had been drafted into labour battalions, and by the time the Germans occupied Hungary in March 1944, between 25,000 and 40,000 Hungarian Jewish men had died during their forced labour service.

Axis The coalition of countries that fought against the Allied powers (Britain, the United States, the USSR, and others). At the beginning of World War II in September 1939, the coalition included Germany, Italy and Japan. Other Axis countries included Hungary, Romania, Slovakia, Bulgaria, Yugoslavia and Croatia. *See also* Allies.

bar mitzvah, bat mitzvah (Hebrew; literally, son/daughter of the commandment) The time when, in Jewish tradition, children become religiously and morally responsible for their actions and are considered adults for the purpose of synagogue and other rituals. Traditionally this occurs at age thirteen for boys and twelve for girls. A bar mitzvah or bat mitzvah is also the synagogue ceremony and family celebration that marks the attainment of this status, during which the bar mitzvah boy — and in more liberal Jewish communities, the bat mitzvah girl — is called upon to read a portion of the Torah and recite the prescribed prayers in a public prayer service. Variations of this ceremony for girls are often held in Orthodox practice as well.

bris (Yiddish; in Hebrew, *brit milah*; covenant of circumcision) Judaism's religious ceremony to welcome male infants into the covenant between God and the Children of Israel through a ritual circumcision (removal of the foreskin of the penis) performed by a mohel, or circumciser, eight days after the baby is born. Traditionally, a baby boy is named after this ceremony.

Budapest ghetto The area of Budapest in which Jews were confined, established by Hungary's Arrow Cross government on November 29, 1944. On December 10, the ghetto was sealed off from the rest of the city. Jews who had held "protected" status first moved into the separate ghetto known as the international ghetto, which was merged into the main one in early January 1945. By that point, the population of the overcrowded ghetto reached close to 70,000, and people lacked sufficient food, water and sanitation. Supplies dwindled and conditions worsened during the Soviet siege of Budapest, which began in late December 1944. Thousands died of starvation and disease. The ghetto was also vulnerable to Arrow Cross raids, and thousands of Jews were taken from the ghetto and murdered on the banks of the Danube. Soviet forces liberated the short-lived ghetto on January 17, 1945. *See also* Arrow Cross Party.

Canadian Jewish Congress (cjc) An advocacy organization and lobbying group for the Canadian Jewish community from 1919 to 2011 that was instrumental in the War Orphans Project. In 1947, the cjc convinced the Canadian government to allow one thousand European Jewish children under the age of eighteen to be admitted to Canada, where they were to be supported by the Jewish community. The cjc searched for Jewish war orphans with the help of the United Nations Relief and Rehabilitation Administration (unrra). Between 1947 and 1952, 1,123 young Jewish refugees came to Canada. The cjc was restructured in 2007 and its functions subsumed under the Centre for Israel and Jewish Affairs (cija) in 2011. *See also* War Orphans Project.

circumcision Removal of the foreskin of the penis. In Judaism, ritual circumcision is performed on the eighth day of a male infant's life in a religious ceremony known as a *brit milah* (Hebrew) or *bris* (Yiddish) to welcome him into the covenant between God and the People of Israel. *See also* bris.

forced labour battalion *See* Auxiliary Labour Service.

Haganah (Hebrew; The Defense) The Jewish paramilitary force in British Mandate Palestine that existed from 1920–1948 and later became the Israel Defense Forces. After World War ii, there were branches of the Haganah in the DP camps in Europe, and members helped coordinate illegal immigration to British Mandate Palestine.

Hanoar Hatzioni (Hebrew; The Zionist Youth) A socialist-Zionist educational movement established in Europe in 1926 to educate youth in Jewish and Zionist principles and to encourage self-actualization through living in British Mandate Palestine. The Hanoar Hatzioni youth movement continues to exist in Israel and internationally.

Hashomer Hatzair (Hebrew; The Youth Guard) A left-wing Zionist youth movement founded in Central Europe in the early twentieth century to prepare young Jews to become workers and farmers, to establish kibbutzim — collective settlements — in pre-state Israel and work the land as pioneers. Before World War ii, there were 70,000 Hashomer Hatzair members worldwide, and many of those in Nazi-occupied territories led resistance activities in the ghettos and concentration camps or joined partisan groups in the forests of east-central Europe. It is the oldest Zionist youth movement still in existence.

Horthy, Miklós (1868–1957) The regent of Hungary during the interwar period and for much of World War ii. Horthy presided over numerous governments that were aligned with the Axis powers and pursued antisemitic policies. After the German army occupied Hungary in March 1944, Horthy served primarily as a figurehead to the pro-Nazi government led by Döme Sztójay; nevertheless, he was able to order the suspension of the deportation of Hungarian Jews to death camps in the beginning of July 1944. Horthy planned to withdraw his country from the war on October 15, 1944, but the Nazis supported an Arrow Cross coup that same day and forced Horthy to abdicate. *See also* Arrow Cross Party.

Iron Curtain A term made famous by former British prime minister Winston Churchill in 1946 that described the political and ideological barrier maintained by the Soviet Union to isolate its dependent allies in Eastern and Central Europe from non-Communist Western Europe after World War ii. The Communist governments behind the Iron Curtain exerted rigid control over the flow of information and people to and from the West until the collapse of Communism in 1989.

Jewish houses (in Hungarian, *sárga csillagos házak*) In June 1944, three months after Germany occupied Hungary, the Nazis and the collaborating Hungarian government ordered the Jews in Budapest to move into designated buildings marked with a yellow Star of David. More than 200,000 Jews were assigned to fewer than two thousand apartment buildings. They were allowed to leave the buildings for two hours in the afternoon, but only if they wore an identifying yellow Star of David on their clothing. *See also* Star of David.

Kaddish (Aramaic; holy. Also known as the Mourner's Kaddish or Mourner's Prayer.) The prayer recited by mourners at funerals and memorials and during Jewish prayer services. Kaddish is traditionally said by a relative of the deceased for eleven months after the death of a parent and for thirty days after the death of a spouse or sibling, as well as each year on the anniversary of the death.

Kamenets-Podolsk (now Kamianets-Podilskyi, Ukraine) An area under German control after the Nazi invasion of the Soviet Union that was the site of a large-scale massacre of Jews during the Holocaust. In the summer of 1941, Polish and Russian Jewish refugees in Hungary as well as approximately 18,000 Hungarian Jews who were primarily from the region of Northern Transylvania were declared "stateless" or of "uncertain citizenship" by Hungarian authorities and were rounded up, deported to Kamenets-Podolsk and handed over to the SS. On August 27 and 28, 1941, 23,600 Jews were murdered by Einsatzgruppen units.

Lichtenwörth A forced labour camp or concentration camp in Austria that was located in the town of the same name, about fifty kilometres south of Vienna. An unknown number of prisoners were held in the camp under abysmal conditions between December 1944 and April 1945, when the camp was liberated. After the war, the American Jewish Joint Distribution committee received a list of 235 Hungarian Jews whose deaths at the camp had been registered.

numerus clausus (Latin; closed number) A quota limiting admission to institutions or professions. In nineteenth- and twentieth-century

Eastern Europe, Jews were frequently restricted from entering universities, professional associations and public administration.

OMZSA (Országos Magyar Zsidó Segítő Akció; National Hungarian Jewish Aid Association) An organization established by Neolog, Orthodox and Zionist leaders in 1939 to provide for the needs of Hungarian Jews in response to anti-Jewish laws and regulations.

Passover (in Hebrew, Pesach) An eight-day Jewish festival that takes place in the spring and commemorates the exodus of the Israelite slaves from Egypt. The festival begins with a lavish ritual meal called a seder, during which the story of the Exodus is told through the reading of a Jewish text called the Haggadah. The name of the festival refers to God's "passing over" the houses of the Jews and sparing their lives during the last of the ten plagues, when the first-born sons of the Egyptians were killed by God.

Rosh Hashanah (Hebrew; New Year) The two-day autumn holiday that marks the beginning of the Jewish year and ushers in the High Holy Days. It is celebrated with a prayer service and the blowing of the shofar (ram's horn), as well as festive meals that include symbolic foods such as an apple dipped in honey, which symbolizes the desire for a sweet new year.

shiva (Hebrew; seven) In Judaism, the seven-day mourning period that is observed after the funeral of a close relative.

Siege of Budapest Also known as the Battle of Budapest. The 50-day encircling and conquest of Budapest by the Soviet and Romanian armies toward the end of World War II, starting in late December 1944. Pest was liberated by these armies on January 17, 1945, but Buda remained under Nazi control until the Hungarian and German troops defending the city surrendered unconditionally on February 13, 1945. One of the deadliest sieges of the war, with high numbers of military casualties on both sides, the Siege of Budapest also resulted in the deaths of 38,000 civilians from bombings, sickness and starvation, and it destroyed the largest part of the city.

Star of David (in Hebrew, *Magen David*) The six-pointed star that is the most recognizable symbol of Judaism. During World War II, Jews in Nazi-occupied areas were frequently forced to wear a badge or armband with the Star of David on it as an identifying mark of their lesser status and to single them out as targets for persecution.

Szálasi, Ferenc (1897–1946) The founder and leader of the Hungarian fascist Arrow Cross Party, which actively collaborated with the Nazis in Hungary, notably in the persecution and deportation of Jews. Following the Nazi-orchestrated coup in Hungary on October 15, 1944, Szálasi was the leader of Hungary until March 1945 and continued Hungary's war on the side of the Axis. Szálasi had fled Budapest by the time the Soviet and Romanian forces had completely surrounded the capital city on December 26, 1944, and continued to rule over a shrinking territory in western Hungary. He was convicted of war crimes and executed in 1946 in Budapest. *See also* Arrow Cross Party.

War Orphans Project An initiative established in April 1947 by the Canadian Jewish Congress (CJC) to bring orphaned Holocaust survivors under the age of eighteen to Canada. In 1947, the CJC convinced the Canadian government to re-issue Privy Council Order 1647 — which in 1942 had advocated, too late, for bringing orphans from Vichy France to Canada — thereby allowing one thousand Jewish children under the age of eighteen to enter Canada. Between 1947 and 1952 1,123 young Jewish refugees came to Canada. *See also* Canadian Jewish Congress.

yahrzeit (Yiddish) The anniversary of a death as it occurs on the Jewish calendar, often commemorated by reciting Kaddish and lighting a candle. *See also* Kaddish.

yizkor (Hebrew; remember) A memorial prayer recited for the dead during synagogue services four times a year on Jewish holidays. In the prayer, which begins "Remember, God," worshippers insert the names of their loved ones, asking God to remember their souls.

Postcards and Photographs

1944. XI. 11.

LEVELEZŐLAP

a gyereket
el tudjátok
látni. Vigyáz-
zatok maga-
tokra, nagyon
aggódom értetek.
Mindnyájatokat
csókolom
          Magda

Feladó:
Löffler Magda

Nagys.
Pollák Géza

Sajó - u 2
Budapest

Édeseim!
Valószínűleg
Pilis-Csabára in-
dulunk. Zsuzsira
       nagyon
vigyázzatok.
Lakásomról ikel-
miszerint ha van
alkalmatok el-
vinni. Valamit
értékesítsetek, hogy

[Postmarked Budapest]
Nov. 11, 1944
To: Mr Géza Pollák
2 Sajó Street
Budapest

Sender: Magda Löffler

My dear ones. We are probably going to leave for Pilis-Csaba. Take very good care of Zsuzsi. If you have a chance, get the food from my apartment. Try to sell something to be able to take care of the child. Take good care of yourselves, I really worry about you. Kisses to all of you. Magda

Sajnos, hogy az ott
honiakról nem
hallok semmit, de
talán ez is jó. Isten
áldjon benneteket.
Sokszor csókol sze-
rető ismerősötök Magda
Dráva-póógra megyünk
holnap este (?) véggel megyünk

Feladó: Löffler Magda

1944. VI. 16.

Ára 18 fillér.

LEVELEZŐLAP

18 f
MAGYARORSZÁG

Nagy Sándor
         úrnak

Budapest
Péter-Várad-u 8

Kedves Bözsike   16-án

Itt vagyunk Győrybe, most
indulunk, hogy hova, azt csak
bizonyosan sejtjük. Édes
Bözsikém, ha alkalmad
van a gyereket pártfogás
alá venni, kérlek nagyon
vigyázzatok rá, hátha
lesz alkalmam meg hálálni,
ha nem, majd a jó Isten
megfizet. Bözsikém a Horváth-
nénál van valami holmi.

[Postmark illegible]
Nov. 16, 1944
To: Mr Sándor Nagy
8 Péter-Várad Street
Budapest

Sender: Magda Löffler

On the 16th

Dear Bözsike. Here we are in Gönyű. We are about to depart but for where we only have a slight idea. My sweet Bözsike, if you have a chance to take the child under your wing, please take very good care of her, perhaps I will be able to show my gratitude one day, if not the good Lord will repay you. My Bözsike, Mrs. Horváth has some of my belongings.

Unfortunately, I don't have any news from home but perhaps that's a good thing. May God bless you all. Sending many kisses, your loving friend Magda. In the morning we'll leave for Dunaszög [Dunaszeg], where we'll stay till tomorrow evening.

LEVELEZŐLAP

Ára 18 fillér.

M. kir. állami nyomda. Budapest. 1944.

1944. II. 17

Édes egyetlen
Zsuzsikám!
Drága gyerekem
ne haragudj,
hogy eddig nem
írtam Neked. Egyet-
len életöm te vagy
nekem, legyél jó kis
lány

Felad.:

Kiss Józsi
konyha

Budapest
VI. ....

Zsuzsikám! Legyél szorgalmas
kislány szófogadó és imád-
kozzál, hogy anyukád minél
előbb haza jöjjön. Mindenkit
csókolok. Én jól vagyok csak
nem tudom mi lesz velünk. Nagyon
aggódom értetek is. Sokszor
csókolok mindenkit Magdu

[Postmark illegible]
Nov. 17, 1944
To: Mr József Kiss
2 Sajó Street
Budapest

My sweet Zsuzsika. Be a diligent, obedient little girl and pray for the quick return of your Mum. Kisses to everyone. I am fine, except I don't know what will happen to us. I am also very worried about you. Sending many kisses to everyone, Magdus.

My one and only sweet Zsuzsika! My dear child, don't be cross with me for not having written before now. You are the only one I live for, be a good little girl.

Nővérein edes test-
vérein nagyon szeret-
lek benneteket es még
szeretnélek látni
mindnyájatokat millió
szor csókollak. Nagyon
kérem lapom elindítni
Magdus

1944. X. 19.

LEVELEZŐLAP

Nagysá

Nagy Sandor
úrnak

Budapest
Petővárad-u 8.

Feladó:

Edes Zsuzsikám!
Anyukád most messzire megy
és nem tudom mikor fogunk
találkozni. Kicsi gyerekem
gondolj sokszor anyukádra,
mert én mindig csak terád
gondolok és ez tartja bennem
az erőt. Vigyázz legyél jó, no-
fogadó, rendes, tiszta, vigyázz
az egészségedre. Nagyon aggódom a szüleim és a nő-
véreimért; de remélem, hogy
mindnyájan jól vagytok.
Drága Anyuskám, apuskám
az ég áldjon meg benneteket,
ahogy azt Ti megérdemlitek

[Postmarked Hegyeshalom]
Nov. 19, 1944
To: Mr Sándor Nagy
8 Pétervárad Street

Sender: Magda Lendvay

My dear Zsuzsika. Your Mum is going far away and I don't know when we will meet again. My little child, think of your Mum often, because you are all I can think of and that is what sustains me. My flower, always be good, obedient, clean and tidy, take good care of your health. I really worry about my parents and my sister, but I hope you are all well. My dear Mum and Dad. May Heaven bless you as you deserve.

My sister, my dear sibling. I love you all very much and I would like to see you again. Sending a million kisses to all of you. Please forward this card. Magdus

Magyarország jövő békessége és felvirágzása —
a szovjetoroszországi harcmezőkön dől el !

TÁBORI POSTAI LEVELEZŐLAP.

A feladó

neve: ....

foglalkozása: ....

címe: ....

Ára: 1 fillér

Címe: ....

A tábori posta száma: ....

A cenzúrázott csapattestének elhelyezkedésének megjelölése
szigorúan tilos !

Édes Sanyikám !

Üdvözletünket küldjük mindannyi-
an jól vagyunk, légy nyugodt, meg-
....
her.

Szeretettel a hol

Magdus

[This is a regulation army postcard. It bears the slogan: "The future peace and resurgence of Hungary will be decided on the Soviet Russian battlefields!"]
[Postmark illegible]
[Address barely legible]
[29 Nov. 1944]
To: Mr Sándor Nagy
8 Pétervárad Street
Budapest

[Sender: Béla Lendvay]
[23 Kapuvár Street ?]
[Sopron ?]

On Nov. 29th
    My dear Sanyika! We send our greetings, we are all well. Please go over to Péterfy Sándor Street to Géza's place. With fond kisses. Magdus.
P.S. If you know anything about the child, send me word.

1

2

3

1 & 2 Susan's maternal great-grandparents, Regina and Herman Lieber. Nagyvárad, Hungary, date unknown.

3 Susan's maternal family, the Weiszes, before the war. Standing in back (left to right): Susan's aunt Bözsi, her uncle Lajos, her aunt Ilus, her uncle Géza Pollak, and her mother, Magdolna (Magdus). Sitting in front (left to right): Susan's grandmother, Eszter, her grandfather, Farkas, her aunt Ibi, her cousin Bandi, her great-grandmother, Regina Lieber, holding her baby cousin, Ágnes (Ági), and her aunt Malvin. Budapest, Hungary, 1927.

1 & 2 Susan's parents, Bernard Löffler and Magdus Weisz, before their marriage.
  Budapest, 1928.

3 Susan's parents at a wedding where her mother was a bridesmaid. Budapest, 1928.

4 The wedding of Susan's parents. Budapest, 1932.

Susan as an infant. Budapest, 1933.

1 Susan at approximately one year old. Budapest, circa 1934.
2 Susan, age five. Budapest, 1938.
3 Susan and her parents. Budapest, 1938.

1   Susan at around age eight. Budapest, circa 1942.

2   Susan and her mother. Budapest, 1943.

3   Susan (seated in front, left) at her maternal grandparents 45th wedding anniversary. Last row, left to right: Cousin Bandi; Uncle Lajos; Uncle Sandor; and Uncle Géza. Next row, left to right: Cousin Éva; Aunt Ilus; Aunt Ibi; Aunt Magda; Susan's mother, Magda; Aunt Bözsi; and Cousin Ágnes. Seated in middle: Grandmother Eszter; Grandfather Farkas; and Aunt Malvin. In front: Susan and her cousin Marietta. Budapest, 1943.

1

2

1 Susan's whole family at her maternal grandparents 45th wedding anniversary. Last row, left to right: Cousin Laci; Aunt Ilus; Cousin Bandi; Uncle Lajos; Great-uncle Miklos; and Susan's mother, Magda. Next row, standing, left to right: Great-aunt Szeren; Cousin Éva; Aunt Ibi; Aunt Magda; Great-aunt Gizi; Aunt Bözsi; Cousin Ágnes; Uncle Géza. Seated in middle: Grandmother Eszter; Grandfather Farkas; Aunt Malvin. Seated in front: Susan (left) and her cousin Marietta. Budapest, 1943.

2 Susan's maternal grandparents, Eszter and Farkas, on their fiftieth wedding anniversary, after the war. Budapest, 1948.

1 Susan (left) with her cousin Éva and her uncle Sandor after the war. Budapest, 1948.
2 Susan (right) with her friend Zsuzsi Lausch. Budapest, 1948.
3 Susan's passport from Budapest, 1948, before leaving for Canada.

1 Susan and Mr. Jack Klein soon after her arrival in Canada. Vegreville, Alberta, circa 1948.

2 Susan (right) with her close friend Gizi Weisz (Ellen Brownstone) from Budapest, who arrived with one of the first transports of orphans to Canada. Winnipeg, circa 1950.

3 Susan with friends. Calgary, circa 1949.

Young Displaced Person Excels In Examinations

VEGREVILLE.—Remarkable progress of "D.P." Susanne Loffler, of Budapest, Hungary, who, along with a group of other girls, was brought to Canada in August, 1948, has been disclosed in departmental examination results.

Susanne's father met his death in a concentration-camp. Her mother met similar fate at Dachau. Susanne was received into the hospitable home of Mr. and Mrs. Jack Klein, and after attending Vegreville Public School, despite the fact that she was unable to read or speak English, has been awarded provincial department of education Grade "A" diploma in grade nine, making her eligible for advancement to Grade 10.

Departmental examinations disclose the following score: reading, excellent; English, very good; social studies, very good; mathematics, excellent; science and health, excellent.

In addition to the foregoing, Susanne took optional subjects of typewriting, home economics and music. Her teachers were John Finlay, principal, and G. N. Hosking.

The most notable achievement in the class was that of Susanne Loffler who came here just one year ago from Hungary. Susanne passed with an "A" grading, receiving honors in mathematics and science, "A" in social studies and English, and "B" in the special reading test. Susanne could speak very little English when she began her grade nine studies, but would work feverishly during class with her Hungarian-English dictionary. By review time she had overcome the language difficulty and took an active part in class discussions repeatedly demonstrating her brilliance to the class and teachers.

The grouping of gradings in the class is as follows:

VEGREVILLE, Alta. (CP) — Young Susanne Lofflar couldn't speak English when she was brought from Hungary 12 months ago, but she got top grades in all her sujects in grade nine this spring and has been promoted. Both her parents were killed in German concentration camps and she now lives with Mr. and Mrs. Jack Klein.

Newspaper article clippings from the Vegreville, Winnipeg and Edmonton newspapers that describe Susan's scholastic achievements as a newcomer to Canada. Circa 1949.

Susan and her boyfriend, Harry Garfinkel, at a Sadie Hawkins Day dance. Winnipeg, 1952.

1

2

3

1 Susan and Harry, just engaged, at a stadium. Winnipeg, 1953.
2 Susan's wedding picture. Winnipeg, 1954.
3 Susan and Harry's wedding. Winnipeg, 1954.

1 Susan's uncle, Géza Pollak, who did not survive the war. Budapest, date unknown.

2 Susan's aunt Malvin, in her passport photo before coming to Canada, circa 1960.

3 Susan's cousins Frici (Fred) and Ágnes (Ági), and their children, Kathy and George, on their way to Canada. 1957.

4 Susan's aunt Malvin and cousins Fred, Ági and George. Winnipeg, circa 1965.

1

2

1   Susan's relatives who came from Hungary after the revolution. From left to right, her cousin Edith, her cousin Susan (who was named after her) and her cousin Kathy. Winnipeg, 1960s.

2   Left to right: Susan's cousin Edith; Susan; her cousin Susan; and her friend Kathy Blum Griesz. Winnipeg, 1970s.

Susan's graduation from the University of Winnipeg with a bachelor of arts (honours). Winnipeg, 1975.

Susan and Harry celebrating his 65th birthday. Winnipeg, circa 1988.

Susan (right) at the reunion of her friends from the transport of war orphans from Hungary in 1948. On the left is Kitty Salsberg; in the centre is Stephen Nasser. Toronto, circa 2007.

3

1 Susan's children, David, Shelley and Gail (in front), at the bat mitzvah of Susan's granddaughter Ashley. Winnipeg, March 10, 2006.

2 Susan, centre, with her granddaughter Michelle and her daughter Gail. Winnipeg, 2009.

3 The family of Susan's daughter Gail Halbrich at Ashley's bat mitzvah. In back, Michelle and Gail; in front, Alon and David. Winnipeg, March 10, 2006.

Susan (centre) with her grandchildren. From left to right: Michelle, Ashley, Lauren, Susan, Matthew, Hart and Alon. Winnipeg, 2010.

1 The family of Susan's daughter Shelley Garfield. From left to right: Lauren, David, Shelley and Ashley. Toronto, 2013.

2 Susan with her granddaughters Ashley and Lauren. Mexico, 2015.

3 The family of Susan's son, David Garfield, at Hart's graduation from the University of Manitoba. From left to right: Matthew, David, Hart and Carole. Winnipeg, June 8, 2018.

4 Susan with Matthew and Hart at his graduation. Winnipeg, 2018.

Susan's grandson Alon and granddaughter-in-law, Lori, with their children, Lia and Evan. Tel Aviv, Israel, 2018.

Susan on her 85th birthday. Winnipeg, June 3, 2018.

Index